Cambridge E

MW00527119

Elements in Criminology
edited by
David Weisburd
George Mason University, Virginia

WHOSE 'EYES ON THE STREET' CONTROL CRIME?

Expanding Place Management into Neighborhoods

Shannon J. Linning
Simon Fraser University

John E. Eck
University of Cincinnati

CAMBRIDGE
UNIVERSITY PRESS

CAMBRIDGE
UNIVERSITY PRESS

University Printing House, Cambridge CB2 8BS, United Kingdom

One Liberty Plaza, 20th Floor, New York, NY 10006, USA

477 Williamstown Road, Port Melbourne, VIC 3207, Australia

314–321, 3rd Floor, Plot 3, Splendor Forum, Jasola District Centre, New Delhi – 110025, India

103 Penang Road, #05–06/07, Visioncrest Commercial, Singapore 238467

Cambridge University Press is part of the University of Cambridge.

It furthers the University's mission by disseminating knowledge in the pursuit of education, learning, and research at the highest international levels of excellence.

www.cambridge.org
Information on this title: www.cambridge.org/9781108949330
DOI: 10.1017/9781108954143

First published 2021

A catalogue record for this publication is available from the British Library.

ISBN 978-1-108-94933-0 Paperback
ISSN 2633-3341 (online)
ISSN 2633-3333 (print)

Whose 'Eyes on the Street' Control Crime?

Expanding Place Management into Neighborhoods

Elements in Criminology

DOI: 10.1017/9781108954143
First published online: October 2021

Shannon J. Linning
Simon Fraser University

John E. Eck
University of Cincinnati

Author for correspondence: Shannon J. Linning, shannon_linning@sfu.ca

Abstract: Jane Jacobs coined the phrase *eyes on the street* to depict those who maintain order in cities. Most criminologists assume these eyes belong to residents. In this Element we show that most of the eyes she described belonged to shopkeepers and property owners. They, along with governments, wield immense power through property ownership and regulation. From her work, we propose a Neo-Jacobian perspective to reframe how crime is connected to neighborhood function through deliberate decision-making at places. It advances three major turning points for criminology. This includes turns from: 1. residents to place managers as the primary source of informal social control; 2. ecological processes to outsiders' deliberate actions that create crime opportunities; and 3. a top-down macro- to bottom-up micro-spatial explanation of crime patterns. This perspective demonstrates the need for criminology to integrate further into economics, political science, urban planning, and history to improve crime control policies.

Keywords: Jane Jacobs, crime at place, place management, hot spots, property ownership, urban planning, community criminology, neighborhoods, informal social control

ISBNs: 9781108949330 (PB), 9781108954143 (OC)
ISSNs: 2633-3341 (online), 2633-3333 (print)

Contents

1 Trouble Seeing: The Community, Place, and Crime Problem

The Barksdale Market, as we will call it, was the most popular store on the block, yet few shopped there. From the street you would see a mom-and-pop convenience store that sold sugary beverages, snack foods, lottery tickets, and cigarettes. But the owner did not earn much of his revenue from the sale of these goods. Inside you would see that many of the items, long past their expiration dates, were amassing dust. Instead, the store was the hub of a retail drug market, the center of an organized shoplifting enterprise, a money laundering front, and the nucleus for street robberies on the surrounding blocks.

The blocks surrounding the Barksdale were some of the least popular in the city. Many buildings were vacant and several had plywood covering broken windows. Trash cans sprinkled along the sidewalks were always overflowing and litter was scattered around. Lettering from the signage above several storefronts had fallen off. Graffiti appeared on many of the buildings. Men loitered in the area but had little to do. In fact, the few who seemed to benefit most from the disorder on these blocks were the local drug dealers. They worked in tandem with the owner of the Barksdale because of its favorable location.

The Barksdale was close to a central intersection in Walnut Hills, a neighborhood located a couple miles northeast of downtown Cincinnati, Ohio. It saw ample automobile and foot traffic. Two bus routes stopped near the front of the store and two other routes had stops a block away. It was near an alley that connected a commuter street to a lane behind the store. Across the street were two major franchise businesses, a pharmacy and a grocery store, surrounded by a paved parking lot. Drug dealers could sell easily near the Barksdale: by the bus stop in front, in the alley to the side, and in the parking lot across the street. The Barksdale's owner got a cut. He stored the drugs, laundered the money, and stashed the weapons behind the seemingly conventional goods sitting on the shelves. But the dusty goods had nefarious origins too. When drug users had no money to purchase drugs, the owner traded money for goods users had shoplifted from the pharmacy and grocery store across the street. Laundry detergent, for example. The Barksdale's owner then placed these items on his shelves at discount prices.

The owner's business model was sustainable for quite some time. Yet today the Barksdale is gone and crime at and around the property is almost nonexistent. In fact, crime in the area is the lowest it has been in decades (Linning, 2019). If you walked down the same block today, you would never guess the story we have just told. So what happened?

The police department appointed a new district captain to oversee policing efforts in the neighborhood. He was troubled by the Barksdale and several other properties nearby. These places kept reopening despite persistent police efforts to close them using raids and many arrests of local offenders. The new captain understood the secret to these criminal enterprises: property rights and the powers of ownership. They could sustain their criminal activities because they controlled the infrastructure needed to do so. No number of arrested dealers could touch these owners. No number of door-kicking raids could displace them. Even if they were arrested, they could transfer ownership to a confederate and reopen with a new name on the door and the same dusty goods on the shelves.

The captain sought to understand the history of the property, who used it, and how. After gathering information from the local nonprofit redevelopment foundation, city officials, and legal records, he discovered that many noncrime related problems also plagued the property. It had unpaid tax liens to the city, but the tax department had yet to collect them. It had several building code violations, but the codes department gave it no priority. It also fell short of several health code standards, but the health department did little. And none of the city departments that could have done something were aware that they shared the problem with each other. When the captain put all this information together, and presented it to the separate departments, the city became motivated to shutter the business.

The captain organized a joint effort with the local police, redevelopment foundation, city, building inspector, health inspector, and a local prosecutor. After another raid, the city seized the property for outstanding taxes and building and health code violations. This dramatically reduced crime at and around the Barksdale, an effect that persists today. Street dealers no longer had a nucleus for their activities. Drug users no longer had a place that would take their robbery and shoplifting proceeds in exchange for drugs. The city sold the property to be remodeled into a legitimate business (Linning, 2019).

All cities have their Barksdale Markets. So its demise teaches us an important lesson: bad addresses can drive neighborhood crime. The redevelopment of the Barksdale and other sites nearby teach the converse: local businesses create much of the orderly activity in neighborhoods. On the surface this may not seem like a major revelation. After all, the crime and place literature has consistently shown that a small proportion of places account for the majority of crime (Sherman et al., 1989; Weisburd et al., 2012, 2016; Wilcox & Eck, 2011). This phenomenon is so common that criminology has accepted it as a fundamental law (Weisburd, 2015). But this literature is largely devoid of how crime at places influences crime in adjacent areas. Place management theory (Eck, 1994) is the only explanation we currently have to account for the criminal activity occurring at places. But the theory provides little insight into the wider neighborhood influence that a place like the Barksdale had on Walnut Hills.

Community criminology should explain this but does not. Macrolevel theories seek to explain why some large geographic areas – like neighborhoods – have more crime than others (Sampson, 2012; Shaw & McKay, 1942; Taylor, 2015; Wilcox et al., 2018). However, this research is unable to account for why high crime places exist within neighborhoods (Eck, 2018). Recent works that integrate place and neighborhood theories try to explain this. They offer a top-down approach whereby wider neighborhood effects influence offenders' microspatial target selection decisions (Tillyer et al., 2021; Wilcox & Tillyer, 2018).

But the Barksdale Market example suggests the reverse: a bottom-up process whereby criminal activity originates at places and radiates out to the surrounding areas. Evidence for a bottom-up process has been emerging for some time (Weisburd et al., 2006). Clarke and Weisburd's (1994) diffusion of crime control benefits paper showed that crime reductions at hot spots often drive down crime at nearby places (for other examples, see Anaheim Police Department, 2007; Edmonton Police Service, 1995; Royal Canadian Mounted Police, 2002). Systematic reviews and meta-analyses have demonstrated the prevalence of the diffusion insight (Bowers et al., 2011; Braga et al., 2019; Guerette & Bowers, 2009). Bowers' (2014) analysis of thefts in the United Kingdom found that "risky facilities act as crime 'radiators', causing crime in the immediate environment as well as internally" (p. 389).

This evidence suggests that the impact the Barksdale had on its surroundings is not unique. Walnut Hills had several crime radiators like the Barksdale. They have since been systematically shut down, renovated, and restored as legitimate businesses. Linning (2019) demonstrated that these efforts reduced crime. Studying Walnut Hills indicated that what was going on was more than just shutting down hot addresses. It revealed a network of people and organizations that criminologists seldom discuss. The more we learned about who was enacting these changes and how, the more we realized that no criminological theories could fully account for what we were seeing. We had to pay attention to processes criminologists do not typically examine: redevelopment, property finance, urban planning, and history.

Prior to these changes, Walnut Hills was one of the poorest and most violent neighborhoods in Cincinnati (Gerard, 2016; Ghosh et al., 2009). It had some active businesses and many derelict buildings and vacant properties. The nonprofit Walnut Hills Redevelopment Foundation (WHRF) decided to hire a new director who sought to transform the neighborhood. Short on funds, he decided to do this one place at a time, beginning along the neighborhood's three-quarter mile business corridor (Copsey, 2018; Wright & Nickol, 2016). The director lived in another state and the resources the WHRF depended upon to accomplish the changes came mostly from outside the neighborhood. He claimed that if the WHRF succeeded in redeveloping a few key addresses on a few key street segments, the benefits would permeate to the surrounding neighborhood.

The WHRF planned to work with property owners and developers. It would use local, state, and federal incentives found in various tax and financing laws to create incentives for redevelopment by public and private entities. This would underwrite the restoration of old buildings, converting them from abandoned shells to useful businesses and residences. And this would draw people onto the main streets of the neighborhood, helping the businesses thrive, making more restoration feasible, and encouraging further investment. The WHRF also did serious work with residents. It hired local people and solicited residents' opinions on development (WHRF, 2016), but this was to mitigate anticipated side effects and avoid harmful decisions. Though consulted, residents did not drive the redevelopment.

We were able to see much of the process firsthand. John had just moved into an adjacent neighborhood in the spring of 2015 just as the first few projects were starting. By chance, he saw the WHRF director present about his place-based strategy to transform the neighborhood. Intrigued by this approach, he wondered, would it work? If it did, what lessons could it provide about communities, places, and crime? Here was an opportunity to see a neighborhood change in real time. In the fall, Shannon began her doctoral studies at the University of Cincinnati. After conversations with John about the neighborhood she decided that she wanted to answer these and other questions. She gathered crime data from the police department and property data from the city and county. She interviewed people closely tied to the neighborhood, including property owners and developers, business owners, residents, police officials, and city employees. We both attended community meetings and neighborhood clean ups, and patronized the coffee shops, restaurants, bars, and stores in the neighborhood as they opened. We walked the streets with the active redevelopment, and the residential streets that were untouched.

Over the four years that we studied Walnut Hills, redevelopment projects grew rapidly. The place-based approach appeared to be working. Increasing numbers of people from outside the neighborhood frequented the street segments where WHRF focused its resources. It gained a reputation as a new vibrant area to relax, work, and live (Demeropolis, 2019; Rogers, 2018; Tweh,

2016). Walnut Hills shed its reputation as a drive through neighborhood and became a drive to neighborhood. The neighborhood felt safer to us, and judging from the increased use of the area, it seemed to feel safer to many others. The police department also observed a decline in crime (Linning, 2019).

It became apparent that Walnut Hills was not transforming via natural, ecological processes. Neither were greater changes in other Cincinnati neighborhoods that had started down this path earlier (Woodard, 2016). We saw little indication in community meetings, public functions, or in the news that residents had become more cohesive, more trusting of one another, or had greater expectations that their neighbors would act to preserve order. Attendance at community safety meetings showed little noticeable increases. Yet, crime declined.

The business and property owners seemed to be having the biggest impact. Shannon's interviews revealed a network of place managers – namely owners and delegated managers of property (Eck, 1994) – who were working together to improve the neighborhood. Property developers controlled blocks by purchasing vacant buildings and problem properties, like the Barksdale. They redeveloped them and carefully vetted the business owners to whom they would lease their storefronts. Ambitious first-time business owners were drawn to the neighborhood because rents were affordable and Walnut Hills was developing a reputation as an up-and-coming area. Established owners welcomed them, while also keeping tabs on their activities. Many owners were on a first-name basis with one another. They engaged in problem-solving together, kept watch of each other's properties during off hours, and shared security camera footage. They had a working knowledge of the problem places in the neighborhood and worked with the WHRF and police. They wanted to establish and maintain profitable businesses. To achieve this, they had to create a safe neighborhood with unique amenities. This would attract more customers to their stores and tenants to their residential units (Linning, 2019).

The more we learned, the more we realized our criminological background was inadequate. Community criminology theories could not explain the concentration of crime within neighborhoods. We saw few residents involved in the widespread changes compared to property owners. We saw the closing of problematic places, like the Barksdale, having a large impact on crime throughout the neighborhood. The impacts were also greater than place-based theories suggested. We met people who were not residents who influenced neighborhood change at the place level. And these people were part of a wider network that spanned the city.

With criminological theory being an inadequate guide, we looked to the urban planning, architecture, and business literature for insight. The works in these fields came closer to explaining the processes we were observing, but there was one problem: these works seldom discussed crime. Another dark tunnel, but it had one glimmer of light. We noted that scholars outside criminology made repeated reference to architectural journalist Jane Jacobs. She was one of the few who explicitly discussed city processes and crime. Her seminal book, *The Death and Life of Great American Cities* (1961), shaped a turning point in urban planning. Scholars in that field heralded her for helping to kill off ineffective planning theory and practices of the 1930s through 1960s (Kanigel, 2016; Page, 2011; Siegel, 2016).

All we knew about Jacobs was what a few criminologists said about her. Namely, that she said we should design buildings in such a way that it creates "eyes on the street" whereby *residents* can survey their streets and intervene when unwanted behavior occurs (Browning et al., 2017a, 2017b; Hope, 1995; Mawby, 1977; Mayhew, 1981; Taylor & Gottfredson, 1986; Wortley & Townsley, 2016; Wilcox et al., 2018). We decided to give *Death and Life* a try. This led us to her writings preceding and after *Death and Life*. Throughout her works, Jacobs wrote about city processes and order. She was articulate, direct, and did not shy away from boldly challenging mainstream thinking in 1950's urban planning. But much of what we read in *Death and Life* conflicted with what criminologists discussed about her work. We saw little evidence in Jacobs' writing suggesting that *residents* were the primary actors to self-police the streets. Instead, we found numerous examples where Jacobs described *shopkeepers*, *property owners*, and *government agencies* intervening in the happenings of the street. This included anything from disputes between people to the purchase and purposeful redevelopment of buildings. Residents were absent from most of Jacobs' examples. The "eyes on the street" referred to shopkeepers and property owners (Duneier, 1999; Linning, 2019; Manshel, 2020).

We discovered that Jacobs did not foreshadow defensible space or ecological theories, as many have asserted (Browning et al., 2017a; Cozens, 2008; Mawby, 2017; Merry, 1981; Taylor & Gottfredson, 1986). Instead, she foreshadowed a form of place management theory (Linning, 2019). Reading beyond *Death and Life's* three early chapters on sidewalk safety and delving into Jacobs' other writings, it became clear that Jacobs had made an economic argument of city functioning based on the economies of street segments and addresses. She created a bottom-up theory of city processes. Places matter to the functioning of streets, neighborhoods, and cities. Those who own places control them. The owners and their places are embedded in large-scale political-economic processes. This puts them in networks of other owners, financial institutions, and government regulators. It means that a small number of elites with money and power could control a neighborhood's places and therefore a neighborhood's crime opportunities. This is exactly what we were observing in Walnut Hills and several other neighborhoods in Cincinnati (Linning, 2019; Woodard, 2016). Our observations suggested Jacobs' works provide a new perspective linking place management to crime patterns across large areas within cities.

The fact that Jacobs' 1950's New York-based insights had currency seventy years later in Cincinnati suggests that her relevance to criminology is more than a few misplaced eyes. In this Element, we show that Jacobs provided invaluable insights to understanding crime at places and in neighborhoods. In Jacobs' (1961) arguments, safer streets depend on the density of small businesses. These draw people to the street. This provides economic resources. Shopkeepers watch these people. In over forty-five years of writing, Jacobs clung to the idea that shopkeepers are the optimal street watchers (Jacobs, 1956, 1961, 1969, 1985, 2000). She saw the centrality of what we now call microplaces (Weisburd, 2015) decades before criminologists realized their importance. For her, places were not merely potential loci for crime; they were the foundation of urban dynamics and macrolevel processes.

Widening our focus from residents to include owners and managers provides a very different explanation of spatial crime patterns. We call this a Neo-Jacobian perspective. It is a *perspective* because it offers a new way to understand crime. It is also a perspective of crime opportunities, not criminal propensity. It is not a theory specifying variables that will lead to particular outcomes. It provides a framework for creating such theories. It is *Jacobian* because it is based on the work of Jane Jacobs, not the Chicago School. And it is *Neo* because it provides a new way of integrating Jacobs into criminology. The Neo-Jacobian perspective links place management at addresses to their influence on street segments and larger areas. It explains how the influence of specific places radiate to larger areas. It provides a bottom-up framework; control at addresses helps give rise to control along street segments that then produces larger area effects. It also aligns criminology with adjacent disciplines of geography, urban planning and architecture, history, economics, and political science.

The Neo-Jacobian perspective provides three turning points for criminologists. But to understand our turning points, we need to reintroduce Jacobs' work first. Although Jacobs is not new to criminology, we argue, in Section 2, criminologists overlooked fundamental aspects of her arguments. We demonstrate that criminologists used a Chicago School lens while interpreting her work. Seeing through this lens, criminologists assumed that Jacobs described residents as the primary source of informal social control. We provide evidence from Jacobs' writings to show that Jacobs viewed property and business owners as the vital eyes on the street. In essence, using a Chicago School lens created

a "criminological blind spot" (Unnever et al., 2009, p. 396) that caused criminologists to overlook the centrality of place managers in her work.

After bringing Jacobs' ideas into focus, we explain our Neo-Jacobian perspective and its three turning points. The first is a turn from residents to place
managers as the vital source of informal social control. This is discussed in
Section 2. It suggests the need to view cities from a more economic and political
perspective than a sociological one. In Section 3 we review the twentieth-
century US urban history that Jacobs highlights in *Death and Life*. She argued
that governments and private business interests undermined order. Historical
evidence shows that much of this influence comes from deliberate outside real
estate and investment decisions at microspatial places and impacts larger areas.
This provides evidence for the second turning point: a turn from ecological
processes to outsiders' deliberate actions creating crime opportunities. This
turning point requires a switch in metaphors; neighborhoods are farmed fields
rather than natural areas. Section 4 discusses the sources of control that exist
through ownership. It suggests the third turning point: a turn from top-down
macrospatial to a bottom-up microspatial explanation of crime patterns. This
turning point suggests street segments and addresses are the optimal units of
analysis for understanding crime patterns. In Section 5 we summarize the Neo-
Jacobian perspective and its implications for methods and policy. Section 6
concludes with new questions for criminologists.

At times our statements advancing the Neo-Jacobian perspective may appear
harsh. We, like Jacobs, do this for clarity. What makes Jacobs' work so
compelling is the direct and unapologetic way she presents her ideas. We
chose to do the same. Like her, we make ourselves present. Like her, we take
a stance that challenges conventional thinking. We do this to raise new ideas that
may help advance understanding. Clarity can appear harsh, but it serves two
important purposes. It reduces the chances that readers will misinterpret our
ideas. It also puts our ideas at risk, making them easier to falsify.

The Neo-Jacobian perspective is also evidence-based, but not in the way that
criminologists usually think of evidence. Other than the work by Linning
(2019), our perspective is too new to have been tested. Nevertheless, our
perspective aligns with existing evidence in criminology, particularly the
work in crime and place. It is also supported by evidence that is readily available
in other fields such as urban history, as well as in government documents and
policies that influenced city processes. We cite this evidence. Our goal is to spur
discussion and inspire criminologists to examine other aspects of cities that
have previously gone unstudied.

We suggest that it is time criminologists take the turning point urbanists took
so long ago. Our contention is that the eyes who create neighborhood social

control are the eyes of property and business owners, including operators of rental housing and their employees.

Are place managers' eyes the only eyes that matter? Probably not: no more than it is only the eyes of residents that matter. Like Jacobs, we see place managers as interacting with residents and stranger-pedestrians in the production of order. It is hard to imagine an urban world where residents have no role in order maintenance. Although traditionalists have made mention of local businesses, these local institutions have remained on the periphery of criminological thought. Theoretically, place managers remain unintegrated overall. By turning to Jacobs' work to understand social control, we see a road to integrating a variety of local actors in a theory of control. That integration is a long way off. We first must articulate how one particular set of actors – place managers – have an important role in the functioning of neighborhoods. That is the thrust of this Element.

2 Whose Eyes? Bringing Jane Jacobs Back into Focus

Jane Jacobs' work provides a foundation for resolving the problems faced by the community criminologists and crime-place researchers. She is one of the few theorists who took both urban processes and crime seriously and grounded her ideas of order at places. In a sequence of articles and books over forty years, she built an argument of city and national economic success on how shopkeepers and property owners keep people safe (Jacobs, 1956, 1961, 1969, 1985, 2000).

Jacobs' ideas have permeated urban planning. Her books, magazine articles, and political activism made her one of the field's the most influential figures (Flint, 2011; Harris, 2011; Kanigel, 2016). Some immediately embraced her ideas (Rodwin, 1961; Whyte, 1961 as cited in Kanigel, 2016, pp. 209–10). Others rejected them (e.g., Hoppenfeld, 1962; Mumford, 1962). Many of the early dismissals were due to her not being a well-behaved woman. In addition to being female, she was not an academic, and she used anecdotes to illustrate her ideas and challenge the entrenched planning theory of powerful men (Cozens, 2008; Cozens & Hillier, 2012; Harris, 2011; Mawby, 1977; Wortley & Townsley, 2016). Nevertheless, supporters of her ideas overcame the resistors and her ideas caught on. Today, Jacobs is at the forefront of urban planning theory and practice. About Jacobs, Page (2011, pp. 3–4) asks:

> Is there any other urbanist whose ideas more people profess to understand who is less understood? And is there another urbanist whose influence is so widely felt even where her name is not well known? We suggest . . . that the answer is again "no": Many who profess to understand Jacobs's ideas don't,

and many more who profess not to know of her work have in fact been deeply influenced by it.

Page wrote about urban planners, but his claims are just as applicable to criminologists. In criminology, references to Jane Jacobs are rare. As Ranasinghe (2011, p. 65) states, "even when Jacobs' work is acknowledged, many writers pay scant attention to the significance of it, briefly mentioning it in passing, which in many cases occupies a sentence or two at best, a footnote at worst" (for examples, see Sampson, 2012; Skogan, 1990; Weisburd et al., 2012). Many seemingly relevant works in criminology do not refer to her (e.g., Bursik & Grasmick, 1993; Kornhauser, 1978; Taylor, 2015). Some use the term "eyes on the street," without citing Jacobs (e.g., McMillen et al., 2019). And when references to Jacobs are present, they are often misleading. For instance, there is the erroneous claim she was a precursor to Oscar Newman's (1973) defensible space theory (Cozens & Hillier, 2012; Mawby, 2017; Merry, 1981; Taylor & Gottfredson, 1986); a point to which we will return.

To show how Jacobs' ideas can help resolve the difficulties we recounted in Section 1 we need to dispel several misconceptions of her ideas. Therefore, we begin this section by examining what criminologists discuss about Jacobs' work. Then we describe what she said based on the evidence in her writings.

Carefully examining Jacobs' works reveals three turning points we will return to repeatedly in later sections. First, Jacobs set great store in the order-creating capacity of small businesses and shopkeepers. Second, Jacobs saw city functioning and change as the result of deliberate decision-making by neighborhood outsiders. We will develop this idea in greater detail in our third section. Third, she dismissed the concept of neighborhoods as understood in most community criminology research, a topic we elaborate on in Section 4. These three turning points form the core of our Neo-Jacobian perspective, which we describe in Section 5.

WHAT CRIMINOLOGISTS SAW IN JACOBS' WORK

Most people who have heard of Jane Jacobs associate her with the expression "eyes on the street" (1961, p. 35). To many criminologists, this phrase suggests designing buildings to increase the ability of residents to watch streets (Browning et al., 2017a, 2017b; Hope, 1995; Mawby, 1977; Mayhew, 1981; Taylor & Gottfredson, 1986; Wortley & Townsley, 2016; Wilcox et al., 2018). Seen this way, Jacobs is the godmother of "guardianship," a term that entered criminology when Cohen and Felson (1979) introduced routine activity theory. But the term was not taken apart for careful examination until Reynald (2009) showed it had three components: availability to watch, watching, and acting.

The idea of the resident guardian has been present in criminology for decades. Many claimed Jacobs saw such actors as crucial to neighborhood safety. Mawby (1977) advanced that "Jacobs emphasises the role of residents – 'the eyes on the street' – and the extent to which their vigilance, part a result of their community spirit, in part of the design of the buildings, becomes a policing agent" (p. 171). Mayhew (1981) argued that Jacobs provided a "planning approach to increasing surveillance opportunities for residents" (p. 125). Similarly, Taylor and Gottfredson (1986) argued that Jacobs' first principle was to "orient buildings to encourage surveillance by residents" (p. 398). Hope (1995) claimed that "Jacobs believed that modern urban planning, especially the differentiation and segregation of residential environments from other land uses, was under-mining residents' ability to cope with and regulate urban diversity" (p. 42).

The residents as guardians interpretation continued into the twenty-first century. Cozens (2008) purports that her famous term represents a design strategy "whereby residents have enhanced opportunities to 'self-police' the streets" (p. 154). Wortley and Townsley (2016) state that her concept of "eyes on the street" refers to how planning policies can "encourage residents to notice outsiders and to provide informal surveillance of the neighbourhood" (p. 6). Similarly, Wilcox et al. (2018) maintain that Jacobs recommended that "build-ings be variable in use and oriented vis-à-vis the street so as to maximize the ability of residents to provide surveillance – to provide those all-important 'eyes on the street'" (p. 154).

Other works contend that Jacobs provided an ecological approach that foreshadowed collective efficacy theory. For instance, Browning et al. (2017a, p. 758) argued that

> Jacobs' (1961) model offers an ecologically grounded approach to under-standing the establishment of neighborhood-level collective efficacy with respect to the control of public space. As residents are increasingly linked through local routine activity destinations, the potential for emergent collect-ive efficacy, characterizing the neighborhood-anchored network of intersect-ing people and places as a whole, also increases.

Browning and colleagues (2017a, 2017b; 2010) contend that Jacobs spoke of the organization of residents and belief that one's neighbors have "a trust-anchored willingness to intervene on behalf of the collectivity" (Browning et al., 2017b, p. 1940). Some believed this will "bring about either social cohesion (as Jacobs, 1961 had predicted) or high levels of crime reduction (as Newman 1972 reported)" (Smith & Clarke, 2012, p. 300).

Others are vague about who Jacobs thought was doing the guarding. They identify citizens, passersby, or people more generally as the primary source of informal social control. Bowers and Johnson (2017) state that "for Jacobs, all passers-by have the potential to suppress crime by providing natural surveillance" (p. 324) but provide no further clarification on who such people might be. Wagers et al. (2017, p. 345) argue that in Jacobs' work "citizens are responsible for social control," but again provide no further explanation of who these people are. Gregory Saville and Gerard Cleveland argue that "the 'eyes on the street' are of course attached to citizens who must be capable and motivated to respond, individually or collectively" (as cited in Cozens & Hillier, 2012, p. 204). It is impossible to know exactly whose eyes they are referring to. Other criminologists claim that Jacobs encouraged getting residents and non-residents to control the street, although their later discussions rest almost exclusively on the actions of residents (e.g., Groff, 2015; Taylor et al., 1995; Wilcox et al., 2004). It is rare for criminologists to acknowledge the role of shopkeepers (for example, see Browning et al., 2010).

WHAT JACOBS SAID

About Residents as a Source of Order

Criminologists viewed Jacobs as having an ecologically rooted, resident-focused view of crime control. The evidence suggests otherwise. Jacobs argues that shopkeepers and property owners are the primary source of informal social control. Residents appear throughout *Death and Life*; however, Jacobs highlights their limitations and puts far more emphasis on the role of shopkeepers and property owners. Pages 34 to 41 of *Death and Life* provide some of the most explicit evidence of how Jacobs (1961) thought city safety could be achieved:

> A well-used city street is apt to be a safe street. A deserted city street is apt to be unsafe. But how does this work, really? …. A city street equipped to handle strangers, and to make a safety asset, in itself, out of the presence of strangers, as the streets of successful city neighborhoods always do, must have three main qualities:
>
> First, there must be a clear demarcation between what is public space and what is private space. Public and private spaces cannot ooze into each other as they do typically in suburban settings or in projects.
>
> Second, there must be eyes *upon* the street, eyes belonging to those we might call the natural proprietors of the street. The buildings on a street equipped to handle strangers and to ensure the safety of both residents and strangers, must be oriented to the street. They cannot turn their backs or blank sides on it and leave it blind.
>
> And third, the sidewalk must have users on it fairly continuously, both to add to the number of effective eyes *on* the street and to induce the people in buildings along the street to watch the sidewalk in sufficient numbers. (Jacobs, 1961, pp. 34–5; emphasis added)

Given this passage, particularly the third point, it is understandable why many criminologists assumed that Jacobs' (1961) concept of "eyes on the street" referred to resident guardianship and that Jacobs inspired Newman's (1973) notions of surveillance and territoriality in defensible space theory (Borrion & Koch, 2019; Browning et al., 2017a; Clarke, 1995; Cozens, 2008; Mawby, 2017; Merry, 1981; Taylor & Gottfredson, 1986). Later in this section we will show why this is misguided.

Criminologists rarely note the second item in this long quote: the meaning of "the natural proprietors of the street." Jacobs does not state that the natural proprietors are residents. If she thought they were residents, why does she call them "proprietors," a word closely associated with landlords and business owners? Jacobs is a clear and adept writer, so it is unlikely this was an unfortunate word choice. The examples she gives later show that Jacobs thought that residents seldom were these natural proprietors. Her natural proprietors are shopkeepers. Also, note Jacobs' distinction between natural proprietors on the one hand, and residents and strangers on the other. Jacobs suggested that residents and strangers are secondary to the natural proprietors in creating safety and order. These natural proprietors are best equipped to carry out the three components of guardianship specified by Reynald (2009): availability, watching, and acting. In contrast, Jacobs argues that residents, pedestrians, and strangers are often less available, seldom watching, and unprepared to act.

In the five pages that follow this quote, Jacobs (1961) provides more examples of what Reynald (2009) would, forty-eight years later, call guardianship in action. Jacobs does discuss residents, but many of her examples contradict the resident-focused perspective criminologists use to interpret her work. She explains the presence of residents and the role they play. For instance, Jacobs describes her experience of waiting for a bus and a resident, in a third-floor window, leaning out to inform her that the bus does not run on Sundays (p. 38). Jacobs (1961) goes on to say that there are certainly some residents who observe the happenings of the street, notice strangers, and take action when need be.

But she also notes that most residents do not engage in these behaviors nor do they understand why streets are safe. She argues that most city dwellers avoid forming ties with their neighbors:

> It is ... extremely important to recognize that for considerably complicated reasons, many adults either don't want to become involved in any friendship-relationships at all with their neighbors, or, if they do succumb to the need for some form of society, they strictly limit themselves to one or two friends, and no more. (Jacobs, 1961, p. 66)

Given this, there is no evidence to suggest that she foreshadowed collective efficacy theory (Browning et al., 2017a). To the contrary, although a social activist who mobilized hundreds of New Yorkers to fight highway construction in their neighborhoods, nowhere in Jacobs' writings do we find any declarations that she believed that social control is created by mutual trust and expectations among residents.

She also points out that residents are not always present to engage in informal social control, especially in the middle of the day. They are at work, school, shopping, and elsewhere. In one example (Jacobs, 1961, pp. 38–9), she describes a struggle on the street beneath her apartment where a man tried to persuade a little girl to leave with him. When deciding whether to intervene, Jacobs realized that it would not be necessary because numerous shopkeepers came onto the street. She described the shopkeepers surrounding the man to protect the girl. The man turned out to be the girl's father. Importantly, Jacobs (1961, p. 39) pointed out that "throughout the duration of this little drama . . . no eyes appeared in the windows of the high-rent, small apartment building" that contained no storefront spaces beneath it. Only the shopkeepers from street-level commercial properties took action. The residential building was problematic for street safety. It contained no shops with proprietors to guard the street. It contained only residents. And she contended that

> The high-rent tenants, most of whom are so transient we cannot even keep track of their faces, have not the remotest idea of who takes care of their street, or how. (Jacobs, 1961, p. 39)

She notes that wealthier residential city neighborhoods are at an even greater risk because they have "little do-it-yourself surveillance" and thus must hire their street watchers, such as doormen (Jacobs, 1961, pp. 39–40). This is crucial for two reasons. First, blocks consisting solely of residential buildings create dead spaces with little surveillance. Second, it highlights the emphasis she placed on shopkeepers and their ability to survey and control the street. When describing a wealthy area, she states . . .

> . . . a network of doormen and superintendents, of delivery boys and nurse-maids, a form of hired neighborhood, keeps residential Park Avenue supplied with eyes . . . [and] . . . if rents were to slip below the point where they could support a plentiful hired neighborhood of doormen and elevator men, it would undoubtedly become a woefully dangerous street. (Jacobs, 1961, p. 40)

Jacobs consistently emphasizes the importance of proprietors for crime control. She gives numerous examples of shopkeepers creating informal social control over the streets. Part I of *Death and Life* focuses on city design and the importance of safety. In its 111 pages, Jacobs provides 110 examples to illustrate her ideas. Of these examples, thirteen of them recount stories of specific people exerting control in the street. Of these thirteen examples, three recount the actions of residents only, whereas ten of them describe the behaviors of shopkeepers and proprietors. In one of the three resident-focused examples, she describes an area that "had no neighborhood stores and no regular public characters" (1961, p. 123). The area developed a drug problem that residents could not address and despite their efforts the problem worsened instead (see Jacobs, 1961, pp. 123–4). An additional fourteen of Jacobs' examples document that areas with numerous stores are safer than areas that lack stores.

Five years before the publication of *Death and Life*, Jacobs spoke about the critical role of shops. Following a lecture she gave at Harvard University, Jacobs published "The Missing Link in City Redevelopment" in *Architectural Forum*. In this 1956 article, she argued that:

> Planners and architects are apt to think, in an orderly way, of stores as a straightforward matter of supplies and services. Commercial space.
>
> But stores in city neighborhoods are much more complicated creatures which have evolved a much more complicated function. Although they are mere holes in the wall, they help make an urban neighborhood a community instead of a mere dormitory.
>
> A store is also a storekeeper. One supermarket can replace 30 neighborhood delicatessens, fruit stands, groceries and butchers, as a Housing Authority planner explains. But it cannot replace 30 storekeepers or even one. The manager of a housing project in East Harlem says he spends three-fourths of his time on extraneous matters; he says: "I'm forced into trying to take the place of 40 storekeepers." He is no better trained to handle this than a storekeeper and not as good at it because he does it grudgingly instead of out of pleasure of being a neighborhood hub and busybody. Also it happens that most of the tenants heartily dislike him, but he is the best they have in the way of a public character in that super-block and they try to make him do. (Jacobs, 1956, p. 132)

The store, and with it the storekeeper, is the missing link in urban redevelopment. Her Harvard speech and *Missing Link* article, both pointing out the role of stores, brought Jacobs to the attention of intellectuals interested in cities. Her focus on the role of small businesses put her on the path to write *Death and Life* (Kanigel, 2016). Oddly, the key idea that brought Jacobs to prominence went missing in criminological interpretations of her work.

In summary, to cite Jacobs as an advocate of residents being the primary source of order on city streets is mistaken. Residents have a role, but for Jacobs the small business, namely its owners and employees, was far more important. Today, we would call the owners and proprietors of these businesses place managers (Eck, 1994). In Jacobs' theory, they are the "eyes on the street." They produce order on the street (Duneier, 1999; Linning, 2019; Manshel, 2020).

About the Role of Neighborhoods and Community

Jacobs' work fits awkwardly with a resident-focused explanation of communities and crime. This awkwardness is apparent when considering four topics she frequently raises: 1. The deliberate actions at places that drive processes within cities; 2. Diversified land use as important drivers of city vitality; 3. Shopkeepers and proprietors as an important source of order; and 4. The importance of strangers to city blocks.

There is no evidence that Jacobs (1961) agreed with the ecological perspective of city growth. This perspective argues that patterns of human behavior, like patterns of plant and animal activity, grow out of the interaction between individuals and their environment (Light, 2009; Wilcox et al., 2018). Park and Burgess (1925) drew upon this analogy and considered various emigrant and racial groups as if they were different species competing for space. In turn, Shaw and McKay borrowed these ideas of urban growth and social disorganization to argue that cities consistently produce "very similar physical, social and cultural characteristics, leading to their designation as 'natural areas'" (Shaw & McKay, 1942, p. 18). The operationalization of natural areas became the neighborhood, a fundamental unit of analysis to study crime (Wilcox et al., 2018; Wilcox & Tillyer, 2018).

Jacobs did not share this view. In fact, she stated that "neighborhood is a word that has come to sound like a Valentine. As a sentimental concept, 'neighborhood' is harmful to city planning" (Jacobs, 1961, p. 112). She declared that "we must first of all drop any ideal of neighborhoods as self-contained or introverted units" (Jacobs, 1961, p. 114). According to Jacobs, there are only three types of functional neighborhoods: 1. The city as a whole; 2. Street segments; and 3. Political districts of about 100,000 people or more (see Jacobs, 1961, p. 117). None of these classifications fit with the traditional, ecological neighborhood used in community criminology. To keep crime down and enhance safety, she spoke most often of "street neighborhoods" (e.g., Jacobs, 1961, pp. 131, 279, 282, 298). She anticipated the street segment as an important spatial unit over fifty years before Weisburd and colleagues (2004, 2012) brought the street segment to criminological prominence.

In Part I of *Death and Life*, Jacobs (1961) shows that streets are the essential units of cities. She explains that the character of streets and cities is the consequence of deliberate actions, not the outcome of some natural ecological process. Two key entities make these choices: institutions and individual investors. Among institutions, Jacobs (1961) pointed out that banks have engaged in mortgage discrimination (pp. 10–11), thus dictating who can own property and where. She also pointed out the role of government policy that creates the structure of cities:

> There is nothing economically or socially inevitable about either the decay of old cities or the fresh-minted decadence of the new unurban urbanization. On the contrary, no other aspect of our economy and society has been more purposefully manipulated for a full quarter century to achieve precisely what we are getting. Extraordinary governmental financial incentives have been required to achieve this degree of monotony, sterility and vulgarity. (Jacobs, 1961, p. 7)

Individual investors make decisions to purchase property at specific locations and to operate their businesses there. People choose to spend their time at places that have some kind of appeal, and someone else created the appeal that drew them. Thus, street environments do not naturally emerge in an ecological sense. They arise from specific decisions made by owners, investors, governments, and users of space. As she notes:

> A sidewalk life, so far as I can observe, arises out of no mysterious qualities or talents for it in this or that type of population. It arises only when the concrete, tangible facilities it requires are present. These happen to be the same facilities, in the same abundance and ubiquity, that are required for cultivating sidewalk safety. (Jacobs, 1961, p. 70)

The formation of vibrant, safe, and prosperous city areas requires strategic use and management of space. Her book criticized planning, which adhered largely to the ecological perspective (Light, 2009), and was directed at planners and those who can influence urban planners. So her emphasis on choices by institutions and individuals makes sense; she wanted them to make different choices.

As an example of an investor making good choices, Jacobs (1961, pp. 243–5) highlights property owner Charles Abrams (a prominent academic and urbanist). On Eighth Street in Greenwich Village, most investors were opening restaurants. These were low risk investments that yielded substantial profits. Abrams saw art galleries, bookstores, and clubs appearing on nearby streets that created vibrancy and excitement that was absent from Eighth Street. He foresaw a loss in popularity of Eighth Street if restaurant-only investment continued. As people became disinterested in the area, he expected Eighth Street would suffer economically and many restaurants would close. Thus, Abrams "deliberately searched out tenants who [would] add something other than restaurants to the mixture" (Jacobs, 1961, p. 245). Some of his earlier investments included the opening of a small nightclub and motion picture theater. He purposefully created businesses that drew more and different people on to his block on evenings and weekends. Jacobs (1961) observed that convenience and specialty shops opened thereafter because of the increased number of customers on Eighth Street.

Diverse streets, Jacobs (1961) argued, create an "intricacy of sidewalk use, bringing with it a constant succession of eyes" for surveillance and safety (p. 50). She observed this on her own street and specifically refers to this as "intricate sidewalk ballet" (Jacobs, 1961, p. 50). On properly diversified blocks, street use and surveillance is constant for nearly the entire day. Beginning in the morning she observed students walking to school as place managers begin to open their businesses for the day. She observed that:

> While I sweep up the wrappers I watch the other rituals of morning: Mr. Halpert unlocking the laundry's handcart from its mooring to a cellar door, Joe Carnacchia's son-in-law stacking out the empty crates from the delicatessen, the barber bringing out his sidewalk folding chair, Mr. Goldstein arranging the coils of wire which proclaim the hardware store is open . . . . (Jacobs, 1961, p. 51)

She explains that these place managers become the watchers of the street, both for the vitality of their businesses and on behalf of the residents who are gone to work during the day. By the end of the workday, some businesses begin shutting down, while others such as the pizza parlor, bars, and restaurants begin opening. In many cases, these businesses remain open well after midnight and attract even more people to the area.

An investment strategy that favors diversity on small street blocks is the bedrock of Jacobs' (1961) vision of a vibrant city. To her, the best parts of cities were streets filled with an array of businesses that draw people to the streets most hours of the day. Property owners are central to making this happen. They dictate whether a city is economically prosperous or destitute and they influence the behavior and safety of those who live there. However, crime is an indirect concern to them. Their primary concern is the overall functioning of their property (see Eck, 1994, who inadvertently revived this idea). If crime is not a problem at their place, they have no reason to enact preventive measures. However, if crime poses a threat to their business, most owners try to solve the problem.

Shopkeepers make up the majority of Jacobs' (1961) examples when she discussed safety, the disciplining of children, and the foundation of city areas. She pointed out that they have strong economic incentives to guard their streets. Being on a safe street directly influences the success of their business:

... storekeepers and other small businessmen are typically strong proponents of peace and order themselves; they hate broken windows and holdups; they hate having customers made nervous about safety. They are great street watchers and sidewalk guardians if present in sufficient numbers. (Jacobs, 1961, p. 37)

Their businesses are their livelihood and creating safe environments encourages customers to patronize their establishments frequently. Achieving this allows them to stay in business. And in contrast to renters and visitors to an area, shopkeepers have difficulty picking up their stakes and moving elsewhere. They have skin in the game.

Jacobs (1961) frequently illustrates the action of shopkeepers throughout her book. For instance, she recounts the many tasks taken on by Bernie Jaffe, a candy store owner. In addition to running his store, he:

supervised the small children crossing at the corner on the way to P.S. 41, as Bernie always does because he sees the need; lent an umbrella to one customer and a dollar to another; took custody of two keys; took in some packages for people in the next building who were away; lectured two youngsters who asked for cigarettes; gave street directions; took custody of a watch to give the repair man across the street when he opened later; gave out information on the range of rents in the neighborhood to an apartment seeker; listened to a tale of domestic difficulty and offered reassurance; told some rowdies they could not come in unless they behaved and then defined (and got) good behavior; provided an incidental forum for half a dozen conversations among customers who dropped in for oddments; set aside certain newly arrived papers and magazines for regular customers who would depend on getting them; advised a mother who came for a birthday present not to get the ship-model kit because another child going to the same birthday party was giving that; and got a back copy (this was for me) of the previous day's newspaper out of the deliverer's surplus returns when he came by. (Jacobs, 1961, p. 61)

While criminologists routinely use the example of residents shooing rowdy kids from sidewalks, Jacobs (1961) has her agents of social control acting in a far more embracing manner. Place managers take on community roles far more involved than simply running their businesses. Consequently, locals considered storekeepers high-status figures within the neighborhood. Many "enjoy an excellent social status, that of businessmen" (Jacobs, 1961, p. 61). These shopkeepers are the ones who create the dynamics of city streets. They can link people and provide guardianship over the street. Jacobs (1961) refers to those who intervene repeatedly as public characters. More specifically, she argues that:

the social structure of sidewalk life hangs partly on what can be called self-appointed public characters. A public character is anyone who is in frequent contact with a wide circle of people and who is sufficiently interested to make himself a public character .... Most public sidewalk characters are steadily stationed in public places. They are storekeepers or barkeepers or the like. These are the basic public characters. All other public characters of the city sidewalks depend on them – if only indirectly because of the presence of sidewalk routes to such enterprises and their proprietors. (p. 68)

The social role of business owners is integral to Jacobs' (1961) arguments regarding safe city streets. As storekeepers get to know people, it creates a sense of community whereby they can connect people. She also argues that they seem to take a sense of ownership of the streets to protect those who use the space. It also encourages people to travel through the streets to enjoy "the uniqueness and friendliness of stores, [and] the pleasures of running into people when doing errands at the next corner" (Jacobs, 1961, p. 71).

However, there is a fine line between the ratio of shopkeepers to the demand created by users of the street. More specifically, she states that:

Efficiency of public sidewalk characters declines drastically if too much burden is put upon them. A store, for example, can reach a turnover in its contacts, or potential contacts, which is so large and so superficial that it is socially useless. An example of this can be seen at the candy and newspaper store owned by the housing cooperative of Corlears Hook on New York's Lower East Side. This planned project store replaces perhaps forty superficially similar stores which were wiped out (without compensation to their proprietors) on that project site and the adjoining sites. The place is a mill. Its clerks are so busy making change and screaming ineffectual imprecations at rowdies that they never hear anything except "I want that." This, or utter disinterest, is the usual atmosphere where shopping center planning or repressive zoning artificially contrives commercial monopolies for city neighborhoods. A store like this would fail economically if it had competition. Meantime, although monopoly insures the financial success planned for it, it fails the city socially. (Jacobs, 1961, p. 71)

Jacobs (1961) saw storekeepers as a source of both social cohesion and safety within neighborhoods. However, there needs to be a sufficient number of them to create safety.

Lastly, Jacobs (1961) highlights the interplay between shopkeepers and strangers. She was one of the few who did not see strangers as a source of danger in cities (Hillier, 2004). They are integral to city life. Strangers can serve two crucial purposes. First, they provide an additional source of eyes on the street. Jacobs (1961) reminds readers that although some strangers may pose a threat to safety, most are well-intentioned, law-abiding people. During her accounts of her street's sidewalk ballet she points out that storekeepers become the watchers of the street during the day as residents leave for work and become strangers on other blocks (p. 51). These are everyday people who do not pose a threat to adjacent blocks simply because they do not reside on them.

She also argues against the orthodox planning view of creating quiet, open, and empty space within cities (see Jacobs, 1961, p. 37). Instead, she believes that streets should possess various stores and public places to create environments where people want to spend time. She uses her own street to illustrate this saying that the mixture of establishments draws people during all times of the day. The bars in particular assure that a substantial number of people will be on or watching the streets until three in the morning (pp. 40–1). In another example, she explains that a stranger helped a local when he injured himself while intervening between scuffling friends. She believed that when a street can foster strong social relationships between users, strangers will also pick up on the atmosphere and act accordingly.

The second reason strangers are important is because they motivate shop-keepers to maintain safe areas. The primary concern of business and property owners is to assure the smooth functioning of their place (Eck & Madensen, 2018). They may serve an important social function, but they are driven by economics. Storekeepers must make a profit to keep their businesses afloat. Attracting customers is the main way to accomplish this. Strangers are essential; they can make up much of the customer base. Shopkeepers want customers to return and a primary factor that determines whether this will occur, is whether customers feel safe. This provides concrete motivation for shopkeepers to take action in order to assure safety at and around their businesses (Manshel, 2020).

To Jacobs, stores and those who operate them have always been vital to understanding street life and safety. Given the abundance of evidence throughout her writing, it is perplexing that criminologists overlooked the importance of place managers when referencing her work. In the next section, we provide insight into why this may have occurred.

WHY CRIMINOLOGISTS' VIEWS OF JACOBS WERE INCOMPLETE

If Jacobs was focusing on the eyes of place managers rather than residents, why did criminologists not see this? There are three intertwining reasons.

First, criminologists frequently claim that Newman (1973) operationalized Jacobs ideas in his defensible space theory (Borrion & Koch, 2019; Browning et al., 2017a; Clarke, 1995; Cozens, 2008; Cozens & Hillier, 2012; Mawby, 2017; Merry, 1981; Taylor & Gottfredson, 1986; Wilcox et al., 2018). Yet there is little evidence to support this. Newman (1973) only refers to Jacobs twice in his book, and arguably in passing (Mawby, 1977). And although both discuss the importance of natural surveillance and territoriality, they attribute the sources of order and danger to different groups. In defensible space theory, residents are the primary source of informal social control and strangers pose a threat to safety (Hillier, 2004; Newman, 1973). Jacobs saw shopkeepers as the primary source of order. She also did not see strangers as a source of danger (Hillier, 2004). To her, anonymity is a central feature of cities. Most people do not become dangerous simply because they set foot on a street away from their home. Moreover, strangers constitute much of shopkeepers' customer base. Thus, they deliberately attract strangers to their stores. For a more detailed discussion of the differences between Jacobs and Newman, see Linning (2019). Once criminologists dismissed Newman's work (Mawby, 2017; Mayhew, 1979; Merry, 1981), they repudiated Jacobs' ideas. But given how her ideas diverge from Newman's, this dismissal was misguided.

Second, academics and other experts disregarded the many examples in *Death and Life* because they perceived them as anecdotes, thus labeling her ideas as unscientific. This prejudice was reinforced by Jacobs' lack of a college degree and her gender, as can be seen in the quotes that follow. Morton Hoppenfeld (1962), a leading planner, reviewed her book calling Jacobs "the enchanted ballerina of Hudson Street, with a chip on her shoulder, would throw the baby out with the bathwater" (p. 136). He criticized her ideas on the basis that "the writer draws most of her inspiration and daily satisfaction from Greenwich Village" (p. 136) implying that she had not drawn her conclusions scientifically.

In *The Architectural Review*, a magazine for professional British architects, Ivor de Wolfe (1963, p. 91) opined:

> The hand and the high wind are both feminine and belong to Jane Jacobs, wife (of an architect), mother, journalist, and associate editor of *The Architectural Forum*. Egged admirably on by Douglas Haskell, the Forum's editor, Mrs. Jacobs has taken the lid off many honoured modern conventions and made a fool of the planners, prairie, airy, and fairy, with a courage which is stimulating and a disingenuity which is startling. Startling because by means of exaggeration and false emphasis, if not downright prevarication, she contrives to come at the truth in a way that makes the truth seem truer than it usually does.

As an uncredentialed housewife, Jacobs' observations were easy to reject. In contrast, a year earlier, Kevin Lynch, an MIT professor, published a very well-received monograph, still widely cited, *The Image of the City* (Lynch, 1960), based on a sample of sixty arbitrarily selected individuals in three cities. Apparently, theorizing based on anecdotes is fine if one has the credentials and the right gender.

Lewis Mumford's unfavorable review of *Death and Life* entitled, "The Skyline: Mother Jacobs' Home Remedies," slammed her for using examples "drawn chiefly from New York – indeed, largely from a few tiny pockets of New York" (p. 150). He claimed that her ideas "rest on faulty data, inadequate evidence, and startling miscomprehensions of views contrary to hers" (p. 154). Mumford also wrote off her ideas by stating that he "... shall say no more of Mrs. Jacobs's lack of historical knowledge and scholarly scruple except that her disregard of easily ascertainable facts is all too frequent" (Mumford, 1962, p. 158).

Lastly, scholars disregarded Jacobs because she challenged the ecological perspective of city growth. Human ecology was so ingrained in urban planning, architecture, and sociology (Light, 2009) that most had difficulty considering alternatives. Unlike criminologists who assumed Jacobs supported the resident-focused ecological perspective, many acknowledged that Jacobs saw shop-keepers as the primary source of informal social control (Gans, 1962; Mumford, 1962). Mumford (1962, p. 170) denounced her concept of "eyes on the street," saying:

> There is still plenty of variety and domestic vitality in such neighborhoods despite their long decay, but they do not follow Mrs. Jacobs' formula of shops and factories strewn all over the quarter. Her overvaluation of the now archaic street pattern leads to her naive remedy for combatting random violence. And her prescription ("eyes on the street") is a result of wishful thinking. Since when has the idea of shopkeepers as substitute policemen kept even them from being held up and knifed?

Mumford critiqued Jacobs' ideas because they did not conform to the traditional ecological perspective that urbanists had allegiances to. Several pages later, Mumford steers readers toward the human ecology view of cities and attempts to discredit Jacobs stating:

> Despite Mrs. Jacobs' recognition of organic complexity in the abstract, she has a very inadequate appreciation of the ecological setting of cities and neighborhoods. (Mumford, 1962, p. 174)

Mumford wanted readers to believe that Jacobs had a flawed understanding of human ecology. As will become clear in Section 3, this was not the case. Jacobs understood the ecological perspective. Scholars outside of criminology and sociology used it to purposefully manipulate cities (Light, 2009). Jacobs revealed how its widespread adoption in urban planning and real estate was detrimental to cities. She explained how the perspective created negative social and economic consequences and uncovered deficient thinking by renowned urbanists. These issues have since been documented extensively (Jackson,

1985; Kuklick, 1980; Light, 2009; Massey & Denton, 1993). They are seldom discussed in criminology but have major implications (Eck & Linning, 2019). We must acknowledge the well-documented urban history that has been hidden in plain sight to criminologists for decades.

3 What Frames? The Deliberate Action of Outsiders

Lewis Mumford's attempts to discredit Jacobs for challenging the ecological perspective are not surprising. Mumford was one of many in thrall to human ecology. This perspective dominated theory and practice in many social sciences through the middle of the twentieth century (Light, 2009). Urban planners, no different from criminologists, geographers, and economists, drew analogies to the natural environment. The University of Chicago's sociology department, under the leadership of Ernest Burgess and Robert Park, promoted this understanding of cities (Kuklick, 1980; Light, 2009). They and their followers likened city growth to a natural process of invasion and succession. As immigrants moved to the city, people with more wealth willingly moved to suburban regions away from the downtown core (Park & Burgess, 1925).

Within this ecological framework, the so-called invasion of northern cities by immigrants and Blacks from the south occurred naturally, as did the outward movements of white residents; no government policy drove these changes. The new and old residents made their decisions in response to each other. This created or undermined order within a city's neighborhoods. Order and disorder emerged, just as it does within ecologies untouched by humans: sand dunes, forests, prairies. These ideas undergird community criminology (Shaw & McKay, 1942; Wilcox et al., 2018).

The ecological perspective did not resonate with Jacobs. In *Death and Life*, she provided a different explanation of how cities form and evolve. Urban change is deliberate, not natural. It is carried out by private investors and guided by government policy. Rather than the analogy of natural ecologies, Jacobs used the metaphor of farms. Cities exist because farmers create and maintain them:

> Thus far, I have been writing almost entirely about the qualities that work for *inherent* success in cities. To make an analogy, it is as if I had been discussing farming almost entirely in terms of soil, water, machinery, seed and fertilizer requirements for good crops, but said nothing about the financial means of getting those things. To understand why the financial means and methods used for buying the agricultural necessities mattered greatly, we would first have to understand why the crop-growing requirements themselves mattered greatly, and something about their own nature. Without that understanding, we might ignore the problem of how to finance a reliable water supply and enthusiastically tie ourselves up instead with methods to finance ever more

elaborate fencing. Or, knowing that water was somehow important, but understanding little about its possible sources for our purposes, we might spend our substance on rain dances and have no financial arrangements to buy pipes. (Jacobs, 1961, pp. 291–2)

Farmers must make money to maintain operations. So they make calculated choices to improve crop yields and profits. Cities, like farms, would not exist without money. They, too, are about commerce. Cities are founded on some basic human activity: a market for produce, a shipping center, a nearby source of valuable resource (e.g., timber, metal, oil), or human activity that benefits from increasing numbers of people (O'Flaherty, 2005). They are rooted in the political economy (Gotham, 2002). Social processes follow. Cities are not natural; they are man-made. Any natural properties that emerge from cities are small in comparison to what is created.

We argued in Section 2 that shopkeepers maintain order on streets. In this section we focus on people and institutions, typically from outside neighborhoods, who have a large influence on area conditions. In Jacobs' metaphor, they are the farmers: property owners, developers, banks, government agencies, real estate agents, and so on. To understand cities, we need to identify the farmers and understand the decisions they make, as well as where they obtain funds to acquire property and construct their buildings. We should also examine those who facilitate and regulate these practices. Such people are real estate agents, and bankers as well as local and national governments. There are two things we can assume at the start. First, relative to the residential population, the number of these decision-makers is small. Second, these decision-makers are seldom the residents, particularly in low-income areas; they are outsiders. Most of their decisions are economically driven (Gotham, 2002), may not be what residents want, or may not be in the residents' best interests.

For Jacobs, this was more than a theoretical position. Jacobs fought one of the most famous farmers, Robert Moses. Known as the Master Builder, Moses created countless parks, highways, bridges, and housing developments in New York City. He was able to carry out his projects by earning the trust of elected officials and being appointed to high-powered positions in public office, such as parks commissioner and the planning commissioner (Caro, 1974). Jacobs (1961, p. 131) noted that:

Robert Moses . . . has made an art of using control of public money to get his way with those whom the voters elect and depend on to represent their frequently opposing interests. This is, of course, in other guises, an old, sad story of democratic government. The art of negating the power of votes with the power of money can be practiced just as effectively by honest public administrators as by dishonest representatives of purely private interests.

Moses consistently gave automobiles priority over other urban needs, even if it meant razing neighborhoods. He used governmental powers of eminent domain to acquire property and evict thousands of residents to make room for highway construction (Caro, 1974; Flint, 2011). His accomplishments repeatedly showed that the will and action of a single decision-maker can impact the lives of thousands of residents. Near the end of Moses' long career of shaping New York City, Jacobs was able to successfully stop him from building a road through Washington Square Park in Greenwich Village and the Lower Manhattan Expressway to facilitate high-speed car travel between the Hudson and East rivers (Flint, 2011; Kanigel, 2016). Both projects would have split Jacobs' own neighborhood into separate pieces.

But Robert Moses was not unique. Moses received the most attention because he was a controversial figure in an exceptionally large city (Caro, 1974). All cities have Moses-like figures. While they may not necessarily be controversial, they are certainly influential. Flint (2011, p. 19) notes that "the man at the helm in Philadelphia was Edmund Bacon, who held the same czar-like position as Robert Moses in New York." At the same time William L. Slayton was in Washington D.C., as was James Rouse in Baltimore, and Trammell Crow in Dallas, among others (Gillette Jr., 1999; Kanigel, 2016; Sobel, 1989). Such figures possess immense control over cities because federal government legislation, local politics, and real estate policies allow and incentivize them to invest in property development.

In this section, we describe the history of cities that Jacobs highlighted. It uncovers how outsiders like Moses can obtain much control over areas. Examined from an economic and political perspective, it tells a different story than the one told by the inheritors of the Chicago School (Kuklick, 1980; Light, 2009; Philpott, 1978; Rothstein, 2017). Instead, government legislation, lending policies, and real estate practices placed strict controls over where certain groups of people could and could not live and which areas received economic investment (Abrams, 1955; Henderson, 2000; Hillier, 2003; Jackson, 1985; Massey & Denton, 1993; Rothstein, 2017; Trounstine, 2018; Weimer & Hoyt, 1948). It was not natural. This history suggests that local and federal government policies, lending agencies, real estate agents, and urban planners created the structural conditions criminologists typically link to neighborhood crime (Eck & Linning, 2019; Jackson, 1985; Massey & Denton, 1993). These individuals created and controlled neighborhoods via four factors: 1. Zoning and restrictive covenants; 2. Government intervention in the housing market; 3. Expanding infrastructure; and 4. Urban renewal. Each was purposefully planned and executed by outsiders. And as we will show, race had the biggest impact in shaping decision-making in each of these four factors.

ZONING AND RESTRICTIVE COVENANTS

When governments regulate how land areas can be used, they are involved in zoning (Rabin, 1989). Glotzer (2020, p. 110) states that "[z]oning was a process in which municipal officials carve the city into areas or 'zones' and then designated permitted uses and construction guidelines for property in each type of zone." Zoning shapes cities and influences many characteristics of their areas. It produces artificial ecologies, much like a farmer plants soybeans in one field, corn in another, and removes ragweed from both. Zoning is an ancient government activity and has a long history of entanglement with segregation (Silver, 1997).

By the early twentieth century, zoning became an important tool of local governance at the urging of real estate interests and the new field of city planning (Glotzer, 2020). With the rise of a planning profession, comprehensive zoning became a way to preserve and enhance the value of real estate (Fischel, 2004). Local governments, beginning in Baltimore in 1910, used zoning to restrict where Blacks and other minority groups could reside (Silver, 1997). The US Supreme Court, in Buchanan v Warley (1917), ruled the use of zoning for such purposes to be unconstitutional seven years later. But the decision did not end local government efforts to use exclusive zoning. It was not until 1949 that the last of these attempts were outlawed by the Supreme Court (Rabin, 1989).

With racial zoning in legal jeopardy, governments and real estate businesses turned to other means to keep minorities, particularly African Americans, out of white areas and in designated enclaves (Jackson, 1985). Direct application of racial zoning was unconstitutional, but indirect use was still possible. Governments used zoning to restrict where multifamily housing was available; to establish minimum lot sizes; create setbacks from streets and parcel boundaries; reduce the size, height, and shapes of structures; and to establish where forms of residential, commercial, and industrial land uses could locate (Rothstein, 2017). By driving up the costs of occupying property, the poor were excluded from the most desirable areas of cities. Since recent immigrants and well-established African Americans had lower incomes, zoning kept them out of most neighborhoods (Silver, 1997). Governments also used expulsive zoning to remove so-called undesirable groups from areas that white residents and businesses coveted (Rabin, 1989). This allowed local governments to change the type of use permitted in an area to expel members of an undesired group. A city would zone an area with Black residents as industrial, for example (Rothstein, 2017).

Though powerful segregationist tools, they were not precise enough. A few African American families could afford to move into middle-class and rich areas. To prevent this, the real estate industry promoted racial covenants on property deeds (Freund, 2007; Trounstine, 2018). A property deed describes the boundaries of a parcel of land and can contain restrictions on how the property can be used. These restrictions are known as covenants. A developer, for example, might sell homes with a covenant requiring purchasers to follow the rules of the neighborhood association. If the new owners violate the covenant, neighbors can sue them in civil court. A racial covenant restricts the sale of the property to people of a particular group, thus excluding members of that group from an area. For example, covenants for properties in the Blue Ridge neighborhood of Seattle read:

> No residence property shall at any time, directly or indirectly, be sold, conveyed, rented or leased in whole or in part to any person or persons not of the white or Caucasian race. (Seattle Civil Rights & Labor History Project, 2020, n.p.)

If a white owner, in contravention of a covenant prohibiting the sale of her property to a Black family, sells the property to an African American, neighbors could sue the owner. If the court finds for the plaintiffs, the ownership of the property may revert to the original owner. The new owner loses her investment (Rothstein, 2017).

By 1948, around half of the new the homes in the United States were covered by racial covenants, creating considerable restrictions on where Blacks could live (Clark & Perlman, 1948). In established neighborhoods, if a majority of residents agreed, then all existing homes assumed such covenants. This burden varied depending on where Blacks resided, however. Gotham (2000), for example, shows that in the counties of Kansas City, between 62 and 96 percent of the housing from 1900 to 1947 was covered by race restricting covenants. Santucci (2019) shows that in Philadelphia, properties with racial covenants formed a cordon around areas with high concentrations of Black residences. Jones-Correa (2000) explains that cordons of covenants were common, along with concentrations of covenants in suburbs. Although the US Supreme Court's *Shelley v Kraemer* (1948) decision ruled that racial covenants were unenforceable by state and federal courts, the use of these deed restrictions persisted until explicitly outlawed in the United States by the 1968 Fair Housing Act (Rose & Brooks, 2016).

Two powerful institutions extended and reinforced the impact of racial covenants. First, the real estate industry supported them. Indeed, realtors helped to spread the introduction of these restrictions. In 1924 and 1927, the National Association of Real Estate Boards (today's, National Association of Realtors) put in its Code of Ethics that:

A realtor should never be instrumental in introducing into a neighborhood a character of property or occupancy, members of any race or nationality, or any individual whose presence will clearly be detrimental to property values in the neighborhood. (as cited in Abrams, 1955, p. 156; Gotham, 2000, p. 621; Helper, 1969, p. 201)

Second, racial exclusion was explicitly built into the workings of the federal government. We discuss this in the next section.

GOVERNMENT INTERVENTION IN THE HOUSING MARKET

As the United States sank into hardship during the Great Depression, President Roosevelt's administration tried to spur the economy with a range of policies known as the New Deal. Between 1933 and 1939, New Deal legislation created public works and investment projects as well as new government agencies to carry them out. A high priority target was the housing industry. Prior to the 1930s, there was little government involvement in the housing market (Jackson, 1985). This all changed when the federal government created the Home Owners Loan Corporation (HOLC) and Federal Housing Administration (FHA) in 1933 and 1934, respectively.

At the time, few people owned homes. Mortgages were difficult to acquire. They required sizable down payments and the remainder of the loan had to be repaid in a short period at high interest rates. The Great Depression caused many homeowners to default on their mortgages and the housing market came to a standstill. The federal government created the HOLC to reinvigorate the housing market. It introduced self-amortizing mortgages with lower interest rates over longer periods of time (Hillier, 2003). It also purchased mortgage loans that had gone into default from lenders and refinanced them for borrowers. This gave more people the ability to acquire mortgages and helped those who were at risk of foreclosure to refinance their loans (Massey & Denton, 1993). Given the volume of investments made, the HOLC devised standardized appraisal methods to assess the risk associated with properties they considered financing. HOLC appraisers divided cities into neighborhoods and rated each neighborhood with regard to home loan risk. Their rating system took into account "occupation, income, and ethnicity of the inhabitants and the age, type of construction, price range, sales demand, and general repair of the housing stock" (Jackson, 1985, p. 197).

This appraisal process led to the creation of color-coded residential security maps: from green A-grade areas that were "homogenous and in-demand" to red D-grade areas that were in decline (Jackson, 1985, p. 198). An important criteria for a red area was the presence of poor minorities, particularly Blacks. The use of race to judge property was not new to the HOLC. Historically, bankers and real estate agents discriminated against people and properties tied to the poorly rated areas, and the experts employed by the HOLC came from the real estate industry. The introduction of these colored maps formalized and institutionalized this practice and gave rise to the term "redlining" (Rothstein, 2017).

The color and letter codes were more than a label. The HOLC would readily provide mortgage relief to properties in green high rated neighborhoods. But they seldom provided mortgage relief in redlined areas (Hillier, 2003; Jackson, 1985; Massey & Denton, 1993; Rothstein, 2017). Redlined areas were inner-city areas, typically. The racial consequences were enormous. One study of a sample of HOLC documents revealed that only "one percent of the applications covered properties in neighborhoods described as 'Negro'" (Harriss, 1951, p. 53).

The enormity of loan discrimination grew. The federal government created the FHA a year after it created the HOLC. Its mission was to reduce unemployment, particularly within the construction industry (Massey & Denton, 1993). While the HOLC grappled with existing home financing, the FHA spurred immense private investment in new home building by providing insurance for long-term mortgages. The agency did not lend money or build homes. Instead, it insured eligible loans to encourage lending institutions to issue new mortgages, thereby stimulating home building and home ownership (Jackson, 1985).

Like the HOLC, the FHA wanted a process that would create safe lending policies. Similar to the HOLC, the FHA devised a standardized appraisal system. Parallel to the HOLC, the FHA relied on expertise from the real estate industry. Following the HOLC, the FHA joined race to the appraisal process. The FHA hired several real estate and economics scholars to spearhead this process, including Ernest Fisher, Frederick Babcock, Homer Hoyt, and Arthur Weimer. Many of these scholars were linked to the Northwestern University (just outside Chicago) and were influenced by the ecological tradition of the Chicago School. For instance, Fisher worked closely with Richard Ely who simultaneously served with Ernest Burgess on the Chicago Housing Commission (Light, 2009; Philpott, 1978). Hoyt and Weimer received their PhDs from the University of Chicago in 1933 and 1934 respectively (Miller & Markosyan, 2003). Many of the ideas they put forth show an ecologically-based way of thinking. In fact, in his dissertation Hoyt explicitly acknowledges Chicago School sociology scholars Robert Park, Ernest Burgess, Roderick McKenzie, and Louis Wirth for influencing his work (Hoyt, 1933, p. x). Hoyt (1939) also extended Burgess' concentric zone model in his sector model of city growth for urban planning.

In short, the ecological perspective that was used to understand the growth of cities was used to manipulate cities in several ways. First, Hoyt and his colleagues influenced the general practices of real estate agents by writing textbooks that leading US universities assigned to their students (Helper, 1969). These texts encouraged practitioners to think about mobility, population heterogeneity, poverty, and social disorganization and then to manipulate these factors to optimize property values (e.g., Hoyt, 1963). To real estate professionals, socially organized neighborhoods would most likely contain properties with the highest values and lowest risk. This meant considering the location of neighborhoods relative to schools, churches, shopping centers, relative to major transportation routes, undesirable populations, and blighted structures (see Weimer & Hoyt, 1948, p. 126; also Helper, 1969; Massey & Denton, 1993). "[B]lighting influences include unfavorable land uses and inharmonious groups of people" (Weimer & Hoyt, 1939, p. 88). The ecological perspective had a strong influence on how to address this.

Weimer and Hoyt (1948) contended that "attention should be given to the general social organization of a neighborhood and the attitudes and interests of the principal owners and investors in the area" (p. 126). They advised professionals to assess neighborhoods based on the same characteristics that criminologists use to measure social disorganization:

> Since future developments in a neighborhood will be determined to a large degree by the decisions of the people who live there, it is necessary to consider the principal characteristics of these people in the process of analyzing a neighborhood. Such questions as the following should be considered: What are the typical incomes of residents in the area? Are there wide variations of income? What percentage of the people own their own homes? Which occupations are represented? Are the people of one general type or is there a mixture of income groups, races, and nationalities? How frequently do people move into or out of the neighborhood? Does the general social organization and "tone" of the neighborhood make it a place where people like to live for long periods of time? (Weimer & Hoyt, 1948, p. 129)

These views are echoed in many real estate textbooks of the time. Many advised real estate practitioners to be weary of the influences of "inharmonious racial groups" and the importance of maintaining racial homogeneity in neighborhoods (Kimble, 2007, p. 411). They contended that the segregation of racial groups, particularly African Americans, is the most effective way to preserve land values (MacChesney, 1927; Male, 1932) and that such people must understand the "economic disturbance which their presence in a white neighborhood causes" (McMichael & Bingham, 1923, pp. 181–2).

Many real estate papers and textbooks also explained how those in the profession can purposely influence structural factors that create social organization and thus preserve or increase property values (Groner & Helfeld, 1948). Weimer and Hoyt (1948) informed their readers of the various zoning laws, restrictive covenants, and deed restrictions that could "regulate such things as cost of buildings, types of architecture, setback lines, types of people in the area, and other matters" (p. 127). To them, zoning laws and "deed restrictions represent another effective type of regulation in protecting neighborhoods against blight" (Weimer & Hoyt, 1939, p. 89). Thus, in concert with local governments, real estate professionals used conditions in property deeds to regulate who can own and use properties (Clark & Perlman, 1948; Gotham, 2000; Massey & Denton, 1993). Many also engaged in racial steering, a process whereby real estate agents differentially direct clients toward properties in certain neighborhoods and away from others based on race (Pearce, 1979).

Many of those who wrote the textbooks, or taught the textbook writers, were also hired by the FHA (Miller & Markosyan, 2003; Whittemore, 2012). Thus, their ecological thinking became embedded in government policy. This included ideas about how to manipulate racial and socioeconomic homogeneity in neighborhoods. In essence, this allowed ". . . the FHA to direct the physical and social planning of suburban neighborhoods in America during their formative stages of growth" (Kimble, 2007, p. 410). Scholars such as Hoyt and Weimer became high-ranking officials in the FHA and played a large role in developing the Administration's *Underwriting Manuals* to conduct assessments nationwide (Abrams, 1955; Helper, 1969; Hoyt, 1939; Miller & Markosyan, 2003). The manuals contained the same warning about the "threatening or probable infiltration of inharmonious racial groups" to housing values that the textbooks contained (FHA Underwriting Manual, 1936, clause 1360). However, the FHA manuals were more than just textbook advice, they were regulatory instruments (Jackson, 1985; Rothstein, 2017).

Because of the policies set out in these manuals, the FHA encouraged banks to invest more in the suburbs (Massey & Denton, 1993). Real estate economists at the FHA saw the suburbs as highly profitable and low-risk investment areas compared to inner-city areas. They believed they could create from scratch socially organized neighborhoods containing high-value homes. Consequently, FHA insurance was given more readily for loans to construct new single-family homes in the suburbs (Jackson, 1985; Whittemore, 2012). This also spurred the expansion of infrastructure to facilitate construction outside of the inner-city core. The result was increased racial segregation and inner-city deterioration (Kimble, 2007; Trounstine, 2018).

EXPANDING INFRASTRUCTURE

We have discussed how local elites made choices that formed neighborhoods and how federal policy reinforced and funded these choices. We turn now to a third, but indirect, factor that influences the structure of neighborhoods: the expansion of infrastructure. While housing policy is important, the construction and maintenance of neighborhoods depends on support systems, some visible and some hidden. This includes the roads, sidewalks, railways, bridges, and tunnels we use to move between places. It also encompasses the electrical, water, and sewer lines that provide services to every structure. In the last few decades, it includes fiber optic cables and cellular towers. This infrastructure too is deliberately created and placed (Glotzer, 2020).

Highways are the most visible type of infrastructure and have had a great impact on city growth and neighborhood structure. Automobiles have enabled people to travel further distances more quickly thus allowing them to work further from their homes. Trucks permit transportation of goods to sites far from rail terminals. As the HOLC and FHA incentives took hold in the 1930s, developers rushed to start building the suburbs (Jackson, 1985). But they, and government officials, knew that new residents needed roads to commute from suburban homes to urban workplaces. By the early 1940s, the government had constructed freeways of significant lengths as part of a planned system. After World War II, "considerable efforts were directed toward the planning, design, and construction of freeways and freeway networks in metropolitan areas" (Leisch, 1993, p. 60). Examples include President Roosevelt's Federal-Aid Highway Acts of 1938 and 1944, and later President Eisenhower's Federal-Aid Highway Act of 1956 (Weber, 2012; Weingroff, 1996).

Improving highways into and out of cities increased the demand for suburban homes. However, a byproduct of the construction was the destruction of existing property in inner-city areas. The construction of interstates outside of cities was relatively easy because there was an abundance of untouched land. But these highways were of little use if they could not pierce cities' boundaries. They had to continue into cities. This was neither easy nor cheap. Governments had to acquire land in cities, evict residents and businesses, and demolish the buildings to create space for construction. The areas that were marked for demolition were typically lower-income, and often minority occupied, areas because this is where land was the least expensive and residents were the least likely to have the political clout to stop the highways (Mohl, 2004).

Governments evicted thousands of residents from their homes for highway construction, oftentimes with little to no assistance for where to move to (Abrams, 1955). Highways often cut through the middle of neighborhoods.

Interstate-71 sliced apart Walnut Hills, for instance, splitting one Black neighborhood in two, connected by two bridges (John, 2020). The consequences for Walnut Hills are illustrative. "(B)etween 1962 and 1974, 311 buildings housing 727 families and 39 businesses were demolished to construct the stretch of I-71 between Wilkinson and Victory Parkway" (Hill, 1983, p. 38). Earlier, but across town, urban renewal and Interstate-75 construction projects forced nearly 40,000 residents – 97 percent of whom were African American – from the West End and Kenyon-Barr (known today as Queensgate) neighborhoods (Hurley, 2006; Konermann, 2017). Many of them were displaced to Walnut Hills, only to have to move again when I-71 construction began.

These practices happened in cities across the United States. Jacobs battled Robert Moses to thwart his attempts to build major expressways through her neighborhood. Like many, Moses focused on optimizing automobile movement regardless of how it impacted the areas that were forced to accommodate the highways. As journalist Ray Suarez (2011, n.p.) notes:

> The car is not a neutral actor on the urban landscape. The car brings mobility, and it brings problems. Moses only saw the mobility; he never saw the problems. If you owned a store in the area of the cross-Bronx expressway suddenly a third of your customers were gone and half of those that remained were now on the other side of the highway. It knocked down all kinds of places that were the glue of neighborhood life leaving a world in tatters, leaving pieces of neighborhoods that were no longer viable, that could no longer attract the new residents that helped keep rents up, that helped keep property values up, that made the whole proposition of living in a place or owning property in a place a long term proposition that you could sustain.

The destruction of the economic and social fabric of streets shuttered businesses, removed Jacobs' all-important eyes, and created disorder. None of this was a natural process emerging from residents' interactions.

The construction of infrastructure along with the zoning restrictions, covenants, and redlining decimated inner cities (Jackson, 1985; Massey & Denton, 1993; Rothstein, 2017). But there was more. By the late 1940s, thousands of buildings were in disrepair across the country, cities were losing population and experiencing high levels of crime, poverty, and blight (Abrams, 1955; Groner & Helfeld, 1948; Scanlan, 1949). Federal and local governments looked to address blight through urban renewal, another choice for urban areas by people who lived elsewhere.

URBAN RENEWAL

By the time *Death and Life* was published, inner-city areas in all American cities had deteriorated. For reasons we described above, investors saw profit potential to build the suburbs, leading them to turn away from urban inner-city areas (Jackson, 1985; Massey & Denton, 1993). Aging multiunit buildings, typically located in urban cores, were far less likely to receive backing from the FHA (Gelfand, 1975; Jackson, 1985). This gave banks little incentive to give loans in redlined areas. Thus, little investment occurred.

The federal government responded by introducing the Housing Acts of 1949 and 1954. This legislation created the collection of local programs often referred to as urban renewal. Using federal funds, local governments used their powers of eminent domain to take possession of properties and sell them to private developers to construct new buildings. This benefited those who owned the properties, but not the tenants in their buildings (Jackson, 1985; Rothstein, 2017). Governments evicted thousands of people from their homes and businesses (Abrams, 1955). Those who were evicted were rarely offered an opportunity to enjoy the benefits of the new construction (Gelfand, 1975; Massey & Denton, 1993; Teaford, 1990). Often, they provided little assistance for relocation to those living previously in the area. In many cases, the developers who built the new structures in these areas refused to rent or sell units to nonwhite residents (e.g., *Dorsey v. Stuyvesant Town Corp.*, 1949).

We have already mentioned urban renewal and Interstate-71 and -75 construction in Cincinnati. Many of the residents forced out of Kenyon-Barr settled in Walnut Hills. As Giglierano et al. (1988) note, "up through the mid-twentieth century, black families usually could move only into neighborhoods where members of their race already lived" (p. 173). Because some 9,000 African American residents had been residing in Walnut Hills since the 1860s, it was one of the only options for many of these families (John, 2020). In other cases, governments constructed public housing complexes for low-income tenants. However, seldom was the new housing sufficient to house all the displaced residents (Klemek, 2008). This also concentrated poverty in certain areas of cities. Moreover, they restricted the racial composition of those who could reside in each complex (Rothstein, 2017). Many experienced disproportionately high crime rates due to the poor place management and poor building design (Eck, 2018; Newman, 1973).

Urban renewal was the government response to solving inner-city blight. But as Jacobs pointed out, much of the blight was created because of the government policy and private real estate practices of the 1930s and 1940s:

> Conventional credit will reappear too in a blacklisted district if the federal government will guarantee mortgages as generously as it does for suburban development and for new Radiant Garden City projects. But the federal government does not guarantee mortgages in sufficient amount to stimulate spot building or rehabilitation except in certified renewal areas with an

approved plan. An approved plan means that even existing buildings must help shape the area into the nearest possible approximation of Radiant Garden City. Usually these renewal plans disperse – even from low density areas – between one-half and two-thirds of the original population. Again the money is used to finance cataclysms. And it is not used to build city diversity but to erase it. When I asked an official involved in arrangements for a "spot clearance" renewal district why dispersed commerce was to be rooted out (instead of more of it stimulated), and why business was to be confined to a monopolistic shopping center, imitating suburban life, he said, first, that that represented good planning. He then added, "The question is academic anyhow. We couldn't get FHA approval on loans with mixed uses like that." He is right. There is no appreciable money available today for nurturing city districts fit for city life, and this is a situation encouraged and often enforced by government. We have, therefore, no one to blame for this but ourselves. (Jacobs, 1961, pp. 305–6)

Jacobs highlights the fact that those with money have immense control to dictate what happens in neighborhoods. They obtain this control by owning property. The decisions property owners make are influenced by government policies and incentives. We have discussed redlining, lending, and construction. However, the types of buildings and their design are also heavily influenced by government policy. If a developer will receive insurance on his loans to build a twenty-story apartment-only building, but no insurance if he renovates an old mixed-use two-story building, he is far more likely to choose the former. Thus, many of these policies eliminated the diversity Jacobs advocated for which contributed to a lack of eyes on the street, neighborhood decline, and increased crime.

RACE: THE COMMON LINK

The theme of this section is that cities are deliberately created and manipulated by outsiders. Rather than natural ecologies, areas are cultivated by absentee owners. But another theme has become apparent: race influences ownership and development practices. Governments and real estate professionals created zoning policies and racial covenants to restrict where groups of people could and could not live. These same outsiders manipulated the housing finance system by expanding opportunities for whites and restricting it for others. Governments burdened inner-city neighborhoods containing nonwhite people with infrastructure to serve those living outside cities. And urban renewal legislation favored the construction of housing units for white residents and provided insufficient and substandard housing to nonwhites.

Economics drove many of these decisions, but it was economics imbued with race. Jacobs fought against this. Shortly after publishing *Death and Life*, she testified during a Senate subcommittee hearing investigating government practices that forced residents from their homes for expressway and urban renewal projects. She voiced concern over the "actual, concerted agreement among lending institutions not to loan to certain areas," and that these blacklisted areas were selected "often because Negroes have moved in" (*Philadelphia Inquirer*, 1962, p. 42). She pointed out that "lacking financial resources to help themselves, these areas 'deteriorate because it is impossible to get money for improvements'" (*Philadelphia Inquirer*, 1962, p. 42).

Jacobs voiced her opposition of these policies for decades. Less than two years before her death she submitted an *amicus brief* to the Supreme Court of the United States arguing against governmental use of eminent domain to promote economic development. She pointed out that "African-American and other minority property owners are particularly likely to be targeted by economic development condemnations" (Somin & Getman, 2004, p. 11). Despite Jacobs' efforts, in *Kelo v. City of New London (2004)* (Somin & Getman, 2004) the justices allowed governments to continue to use eminent domain for these purposes.

Nonresident outsiders, such as real estate agents, "defined and marketed racially homogenous, white neighborhoods, as social and culturally superior, with higher property values, and access to quality schools and other social services" (Gotham, 2002, p. 88). Operating within a human ecology ideology that equated species competition with racial competition, they worked to control the movement of groups to create segregated neighborhoods. Take "white flight," for example. This term depicts the migration of white residents from city neighborhoods that were becoming ethnically diverse to homogenous suburban neighborhoods (Jackson, 1985). On the surface, this term aligns with the ecological explanation of invasion and succession touted by the Chicago School. As one group moved in, another group moves elsewhere. From a social ecology perspective, this may be unfortunate, but it is just part of human nature.

However, historical accounts from the time reveal that much of this migration was instigated by real estate personnel. Through a process called "blockbusting" real estate agents would convince white homeowners to sell their homes "by exploiting fears of racial change within their neighborhood" (Mehlhorn, 1998, p. 1145). To acquire properties, they would tell white homeowners that many African Americans were moving into adjacent areas which will inevitably reduce the value of their homes. Some would deliberately sell a home to an African American buyer on an all-white block to create panic among homeowners that would compel white homeowners to sell their properties (Gotham, 2002; Satter, 2009). Other real estate agents hired African American women to push baby strollers down the sidewalk while agents knocked on doors to point out the impending invasion (Rothstein, 2017). Real estate agents would offer to purchase the properties from white owners. The real estate agents would then turn around and rent the homes at inflated prices to African Americans who were desperate to flee the overcrowded ghettos in inner-city neighborhoods (Massey & Denton, 1993; Satter, 2009). Many fought against these practices and tried to persuade white homeowners to not buy into the panic caused by these practices (Gotham, 2002; Mehlhorn, 1998), but it certainly worked on many. Consequently, real estate personnel deliberately created at least part of the population mobility in neighborhoods.

Another misunderstood phenomenon is community associations. Often used to illustrate informal social control and collective efficacy, they have a less savory history. Rather than organically grown by local residents, many were deliberately created by real estate developers (Rothstein, 2017). As Sugrue (1995, p. 558) notes:

> Neighborhood associations had a long history in cities such as Detroit. Real estate developers had originally created them to enforce restrictive covenants and, later, zoning laws. Frequently, they sponsored community social activities and advocated better public services, such as street lighting, stop signs, and traffic lights. During and after World War II, those organizations grew rapidly in number and influence. Increasingly, they existed solely to wage battles against proposed public housing sites and against Blacks moving into their neighborhoods.

The relative strength of community associations in middle-class white areas compared to poor Black and Hispanic areas may be due to the historical asymmetry of external organizing efforts. Such organizing could not work but for some racial prejudice, but without systemic efforts for commercial and political purposes, much of this prejudice may have had less power (Trounstine, 2018). Race was a core ingredient in the decision-making processes that influenced the structural conditions criminologists claim cause crime including the mobility, homogeneity, and economic prosperity of neighborhoods.

WHAT DOES THIS HAVE TO DO WITH CRIME?

If outsiders wield the influence we suggest, then local insiders have less control of crime than criminologists assume. Evidence from urban history also indicates that the causes of neighborhood crime are not what community criminologists suggest. This evidence challenges several fundamental community criminology concepts including neighborhoods, population mobility, and ethnic heterogeneity.

First, the natural neighborhood is a myth. In his history of the creation of Chicago's neighborhoods, Sudhir Venkatesh (2001) describes how Ernest Burgess invented neighborhood boundaries to aid in his sociology school's research (see also Philpott, 1978). Although based in part on surveys of residents, Burgess' neighborhood boundaries also drew on the opinions of realtors and others with a commercial interest in the areas. Rather than a test of human ecology, Burgess used human ecology to guide his decisions about where to draw neighborhood boundaries. Burgess and his teammates advocated for Chicago officials to adopt the neighborhoods they helped establish (Venkatesh, 2001).

Second, evidence from urban history shows that outsiders manipulated the structural conditions that community criminologists believe cause social disorganization and crime. Population mobility did not occur naturally. Urban renewal and highway construction evicted thousands from their homes to make way for construction (Gelfand, 1975; Teaford, 1990). These policies forced residents to migrate to other areas (Abrams, 1955; Konerman, 2017). White flight may appear natural, but real estate interests fomented this phenomenon (Glotzer, 2020; Jackson, 1985; Massey & Denton, 1993; Rothstein, 2017).

Last, ethnic heterogeneity too has been deliberately regulated by outsiders. Zoning and restrictive covenants along with real estate and lending policies dictated the ethnic composition of areas. Racial covenants forbid an owner from selling or renting property to nonwhite persons (Glotzer, 2020; MacChesney, 1927; Silver, 1997). Developers and real estate interests created and promoted these tools (Antero, 2010; Glotzer, 2020; Henderson, 2000; Trounstine, 2018). This reduced nonwhite people's housing options. Few neighborhoods contained properties without such covenants. Nonwhite individuals had no choice but to find housing in these few areas (Giglierano et al., 1988).

Failing to acknowledge outsiders and their influence on structural conditions presents an alternative explanation for crime that has yet to be falsified. As Jacobs describes:

> It is so easy to blame the decay of cities on traffic . . . or immigrants . . . or the whimsies of the middle class. The decay of cities goes deeper and is more complicated. It goes right down to what we think we want, and to our ignorance about how cities work. The forms in which money is used for city building – or withheld from use – are powerful instruments of city decline today. (Jacobs, 1961, p. 317)

The majority of what does and has happened in cities can be traced back to government policies and private (dis)investment practices. The structural factors we measure in surveys of residents, or derive from census data, do not tell the whole story. A focus on sociological factors has distracted us from considering fundamental political-economic processes. Criminologists who embrace human ecology "... ignore the political economy of our capitalist system and the ways it causes economic deprivation and inner-city index crimes" (Unnever, 1987, p. 846). As Pfohl (1994, p. 169) notes:

> Whatever the benefits of the disorganization metaphor, its disadvantages for the socially and economically powerless are significant. What the Chicago theorists describe as natural ecological conflict is really an unequal human struggle over the control of urban space.

Similarly, in his critique of Shaw and McKay, Snodgrass (1976, p. 10) argues that:

> A most striking aspect of Shaw and McKay's interpretation, then, is the absence of attempts to link business and industrial invasion with the causes of delinquency. The interpretation stayed at the communal level and turned inward to find the causes of delinquency in internal conditions and process within the socially disorganized area.
>
> Thus, their interpretation stopped abruptly at the point at which the relationship between industrial expansion and high delinquency areas could have gone beyond the depiction of the two as coincidentally adjacent to one another geographically. The interpretation was paralyzed at the communal level, a level which implied that either the residents were responsible for the deteriorated areas, or that communities collapsed on their own account. Instead of turning inward to find the causes of delinquency exclusively in local traditions, their interpretation might have turned outward to show political, economic, and historical forces at work, which would have accounted for both social disorganization and the internal conditions, including delinquency. Needless to say, the interpretation as it stood left business and industry essentially immune from analysis, imputation, and responsibility in the causes of delinquency.

The correlations between structural variables and neighborhood crime may not be due to some underlying natural social process. Rather, the actions of outsiders, often driven by economic and political gain, may have produced these correlations (Eck & Linning, 2019).

Acknowledging the actions of these outsiders means we must challenge the criminological idea of neighborhoods, who controls them, and how we should study them. Like Jacobs, we argue we can better understand urban crime patterns by studying crime from smaller units of analysis. Although outsiders wanted to influence larger area conditions, they did so by acting upon the units they had control over: individual property parcels (Glotzer, 2020; Rothstein, 2017; Trounstine, 2018). In Section 4 we explain why criminology needs to reevaluate property parcels as the optimal unit of analysis to understand urban crime patterns.

4 Transition Lenses: Building Up from the Place

We have shown that Jacobs' views on neighborhoods differed from the ecological perspective in two major ways. First, shopkeepers have the primary eyes
on the street, not residents. Second, a small number of powerful outsiders can
control neighborhoods through property ownership. Given these distinctions,
there is a final idea to be gleaned from Jacobs' work: the appropriate unit of
analysis. Jacobs believed that the neighborhood was a poor unit of analysis to
study city processes. To her "the conception of neighborhood in cities is
meaningless – so long as we think of neighborhoods as being self-contained
units to any significant degree, modeled upon town neighborhoods" (Jacobs,
1961, p. 117).

Jacobs focused on much smaller areas: units that some today call "microplaces" (Weisburd et al., 2016), individual buildings, and street segments. She
saw the importance of analyzing city processes, particularly economic ones, at
a microspatial scale (Jacobs, 1981). She condemned planners' aggregation of
data to census blocks, because this was of little use in understanding cities. In
her "Downtown is for People" piece, she protests:

> But the street, not the block, is the significant unit. When a merchant takes
> a lease, he ponders what is across and up and down the street, rather than what
> is on the other side of the block. When blight or improvement spreads, it
> comes along the street. Entire complexes of city life take their names, not
> from blocks, but from streets – Wall Street, Fifth Avenue, State Street, Canal
> Street, Beacon Street.
>
> Why do planners fix on the block and ignore the street? The answer lies in
> a shortcut in their analytical techniques. After planners have mapped building
> conditions, uses, vacancies, and assessed valuations, block by block, they
> combine the data for each block, because this is the simplest way to summar-
> ize it, and characterize the block by appropriate legends. No matter how
> individual the street, the data for each side of the street in each block is
> combined with data for the other three sides of its block. The street is
> statistically sunk without a trace. The planner has a graphic picture of
> downtown that tells him little of significance and much that is misleading.
> (Jacobs, 1958, pp. 156–7)

To Jacobs, urban planners' proclivity to aggregate information obscured the
important processes that occurred at individual places. When aggregating,
planners cannot see the decision-making at microspatial units that influence
wider areas. Instead, she demanded we be hyper-focused. If you study the
happenings at microspatial places, you see many of the characteristics that
influence decision-making that change places and their surrounding areas.
Proprietors at individual parcels are concerned about their places, and those

immediately nearby. Thus, shopkeepers work to influence what happens at their places and those nearby. This increases the likelihood that customers will want to use their places and return in the future. If shopkeepers succeed, then the number of people who travel to and from the streets that contain their places increases.

This process has implications for crime. Recall our example of the Barksdale Market in Section 1. The place drew in offenders because of the crime opportunities the place created. It also created crime opportunities at adjacent places and on nearby streets. As a crime attractor it caused crime to radiate out from the Barksdale (Bowers, 2014; Brantingham & Brantingham, 1995). Once the city wrestled control of the property from the owner, crime at the place and at nearby places declined (Linning, 2019). This diffusion of crime control benefits illustrates how safety across larger areas may depend on control of tiny places (Clarke & Weisburd, 1994; Guerette & Bowers, 2009).

No standard criminological theory can explain such spatial crime patterns. Community criminology should do this but does not. It analyses crime at neighborhood levels and fails to account for high crime places within neighborhoods (Eck, 2018; Weisburd, 2015). Although community criminologists consider the neighborhood as the fundamental unit of analysis (Sampson, 2012), there is no consensus as to what constitutes a neighborhood (Hipp & Boessen, 2013; Taylor, 2015; Taylor, Gottfredson, & Brower, 1981; Wilcox et al., 2018). It is very difficult, in science, to study something you cannot define or that scientists define differently.

Place-based criminologists emphasize the importance of studying crime at addresses and street segments (Sherman et al., 1989; Weisburd, 2015; Wilcox & Eck, 2011). However, they seldom discuss the context of crime hot spots (Eck, 2018). Environmental criminology comes close. Both routine activity theory and crime pattern theory embed microplaces within a larger context of other places, street networks, and human schedules (Brantingham & Brantingham, 1993; Cohen & Felson, 1979).

There have been attempts at integrating neighborhood-level and place-based approaches. Wilcox and Tillyer (2018) proposed the place in neighborhood (PIN) approach whereby characteristics of places work in conjunction with the neighborhoods they are located in. It implies a top-down approach whereby wider neighborhood effects influence offenders' microspatial target selection decisions (Tillyer et al., 2021). However, because the neighborhood is still one of the PIN approach's fundamental units of analysis, it still suffers from the ambiguous definitional issues. It also fails to account for the creation of crime opportunities at the place level and the documented spread of crime out from some places. Weisburd and colleagues (2012, 2021a) argue that we should focus on smaller, more articulable units: street segments. They take resident-focused assumptions of neighborhood theorists and apply them to street segments. Their work provided some support for the notion that community-level factors may operate at a microspatial scale (Weisburd et al., 2012, 2021a; see also Hipp, 2010). However, this approach still assumes many of the community criminology notions that residents are the primary source of informal social control. It also does not account for crime radiating from places (Anaheim Police Department, 2007; Bowers, 2014; Edmonton Police Service, 1995; Linning, 2019; Royal Canadian Mounted Police, 2002).

In this section we describe a bottom-up approach derived from Jacobs' (1961) ideas. Her work suggests that substantial amounts of crime originate at places and radiate to surrounding areas. She also recognized that property owners can shape cities using their powers of property control. This too implies that many of the conditions we observe at the so-called neighborhood-level are products of those who control microspatial places (Glotzer, 2020; Rothstein, 2017; Trounstine, 2018). The Barksdale Market illustrates the negative impacts of influence radiating from places: poor place management at one place can create opportunity structures for crime nearby. But Barksdale Markets are exceptions; good place management often radiates safety beyond property boundaries, down streets, and across wider areas. Explaining this is the purpose of this section, but we start with why places, rather than neighborhoods, must be the foundation of inquiry.

JACOBS' CALL TO START AT PLACES, NOT NEIGHBORHOODS

Jacobs recognized the larger political and economic forces influencing areas within cities, but influences begin at the street level (Jacobs, 1956, 1958, 1961). National lending practices and local zoning policies are macrolevel influences on neighborhoods, but only because they influence decision-making about buildings, parcels, and street segments (Glotzer, 2020; Rothstein, 2017; Trounstine, 2018). Legislation at the national, state, and local levels directly influence property parcels: who can own them, who can acquire funds to purchase them, and what property rights come with ownership (Jackson, 1985). Jacobs (1961) pointed to the proprietors, developers, government officials, and lenders as the agents with the most control within neighborhoods. They possess this control by owning property parcels. Ownership gives them the authority to dictate what occurs at places. This gives owners the ability to suppress or create criminal opportunities. The need to preserve their property investment gives owners the incentive to work with other property owners to create networks that influence the political economy of the area, the city, and beyond.

Jacobs foreshadowed many of the ideas found in place management theory (Eck, 1994). Eck's (1994) original theory was an extension of the routine activities approach developed to explain why some places had a great deal of crime while most places did not (Cohen & Felson, 1979; Eck, 1994; Felson, 1995). Place managers are owners of places or people authorized by owners to operate the place. They attend to the functioning of the place (Eck & Madensen, 2018) and their powers to exert authority over a place are derived from their property rights (Eck, 2014). As crime usually interferes with desired place functioning, most place managers suppress it by controlling crime opportunities. However, a few place managers either cannot or will not do so. It is at these places that most crimes arise.

Place management theory provides the only explanation for why crime is concentrated at few addresses. It explains why some addresses have crime and others do not (Eck & Madensen, 2018; Wilcox & Eck, 2011). Madensen (2007) specified four functions of place managers: organization of space, regulation of conduct, control of access, and acquisition of resources (producing the acronym ORCA). The *organization of space* refers to how place managers "control the physical setting of the place" (Eck & Madensen, 2018, p. 642), such as the physical layout of the building. The *regulation of conduct* is concerned with the behaviors managers encourage and discourage. The *control of access* deals with how and when place managers allow people to use their property, and under what circumstances. Finally, the *acquisition of resources* refers to gaining the resources to carry out the first three functions. For profit-making place managers, resource acquisition is essential to operate. An owner of an apartment complex, for example, needs revenue to pay for his staff, maintain infrastructure, pay off loans, and show a return on investment (Eck & Madensen, 2018). For public and nonprofit-making places – such as schools, parks, and public squares – places managers need to lobby for funding through tax dollars, tax exemptions, and donations (Eck & Madensen, 2018; Manshel, 2020). The ORCA functions interact. For example, the physical layout can enhance conduct regulation and together help control access. Most research on place management theory has focused mostly on the first three elements of the ORCA framework. These concepts are linked to strategies spelled out in situational crime prevention (Clarke, 1995), and have been shown to generate reductions in crime (Douglas & Welsh, 2020).

The shopkeepers, businessmen, proprietors, and property owners that Jacobs discusses are place managers. They have legal authority over their places based on ownership, a rental agreement with the property owner, or employment. However, Jacobs emphasized the acquisition of resources. Without resources, places cannot operate. If places cannot operate, streets become unsafe, and cities suffer. Jacobs' saw money as the lifeblood of all city processes, including crime.

Those with money have the power to own and thus control. They usually have the ability to influence political and economic decisions. As mentioned in Section 3, the desire for profits drove the creation of government policies that ultimately segregated every major American city. Those in real estate and lending desired high returns on their investments and viewed Black residents as a blight on their property values. While segregation was good for their investments, it reduced the control Blacks could exercise by thwarting their abilities to buy and sell property. This depressed investment in Black neighborhoods. The political economics of segregation helps explain why urban crime hot spots are often concentrated in poor minority areas; there is less incentive to manage property well in these areas, and owners often live elsewhere (Eck, 2019). Thus, to understand area conditions, we must look to who possesses control within them.

THE SOURCES AND MECHANISMS OF CONTROL IN CITY AREAS

Let's consider four ways the control of places can influence larger areas they are situated in. These are depicted in Figure 1. The simplest case is when a single owner owns a single place. A slightly more complex case has a single owner owning two or more places in the area. But whether the owner controls one or many locations, he is likely to have relationships with other property owners in the area. That is the third case. Finally, these networked owners have relationships with other institutions, usually located outside the area. The two most prominent types of institutions are financial and government. Both can provide resources and both regulate place managers. Let's look at each case in greater depth.

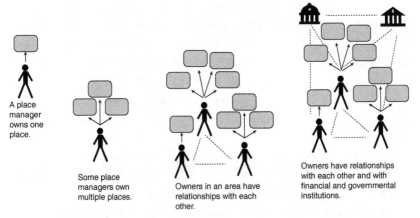

Figure 1 Networks of place control that extend to larger areas of cities.

In the first source of control there is a one-to-one relationship between owners and their places. Individuals engage in each of the ORCA functions to ensure the operations of their single place (Eck & Madensen, 2018). Owners also get to decide who uses their properties. If they own an apartment building, for instance, they can screen prospective tenants and require information to decide whether to allow a person to live there. Similarly, if they are leasing commercial space, they can vet prospective business owners by asking for their business plans, financial support, or references (Linning, 2019).

Owners can also be held legally accountable for what occurs on their property, particularly if it involves crime. For example, citizens who are criminally injured on their property can bring about a premise liability suit against the owner, provided the incident could have foreseeably been prevented (Eck, 1997). Similarly, local governments can sue property owners using nuisance abatement suits when owners allow their property to be used for crime (Mazerolle et al., 1998). Under the law, owners can be held legally accountable for the activity on their property. Consequently, the owners of places are the primary source of control we should look to in order to understand what goes on at any place.

When a person purchases multiple properties, she amplifies her control over an area. This creates the second source of control. Recall our discussion in Section 2 of Charles Abrams' decision-making practices for his multiple properties. Jacobs (1961, p. 245) commended him because he "deliberately searched out tenants who [would] add something other than restaurants to the mixture." This included opening a small nightclub and motion picture theater. In this way, Abrams exerted much more influence over the area than the owner of a single property could. Ownership clusters are very common in cities. Payne (2010) found that a small subset of people owned multiple apartment buildings in the same neighborhoods in Cincinnati. Development companies or limited liability corporations (LLCs) often own clusters of places as well. In Cincinnati, the Cincinnati Center City Development Corporation (3CDC) own dozens of properties in the Over-the-Rhine neighborhood (Woodard, 2016). This happens in cities across the United States, such as New York City (Warerkar, 2018). In some cases, companies own multiple properties in multiple cities or even countries.

The acquisition of multiple properties is a deliberate business strategy used by individual developers and companies. The more property they control, the more profit potential they have. For example, Linning (2019) learned from one Cincinnati developer how owning multiple properties helped his profits. He would start by redeveloping a single apartment building in a transitioning neighborhood. Then he would purchase other adjacent properties looking to renovate them too. When showing units to prospective tenants who were hesitant to move into the neighborhood, part of his sales pitch was to explain what he was doing with the surrounding buildings. He told them that he was in control of the area and its future, that they could be part of the renaissance of the neighborhood, and he would guarantee them lower rent. He reported that this often worked, bringing in many tenants into the area and helping to attract even more.

Another developer told Linning (2019) that he purchased a building that was the frequent site of crime and troublesome behavior. He and his business partners had invested millions of dollars to purchase several properties in the vicinity and saw this nearby building as a potential threat; if people perceived the area as unsafe, it would deter them from shopping, dining, or renting at their properties. So he purchased it. He said that owning it allowed him to take control of the building and redevelop it into more profit-making business space and apartment units. Not only did ownership give him the authority to remove crime opportunities, it also allowed him the power to decide who then got to occupy the space. He made deliberate decisions on which business owners to lease his storefront space to and which tenants to lease apartment units to (Linning, 2019). As such, the clustering of property ownership means that substantial areas in cities can be controlled by a select number of people. Multiple blocks within a neighborhood are often controlled by a few property owners.

Even more control can be exerted when owners band together. This is the third source. A coffee shop owner Linning (2019) interviewed, stated she partnered with the owner of the restaurant next door to jointly guard their common outdoor space. The owners noted that their staggered business hours helped maximize the amount of surveillance for each other's properties. While the coffee shop opened at 6:30 a.m. and closed at 6:30 p.m., the restaurant opened at 11 a.m., but remained open until 10 p.m. By agreeing to keep watch over each other's properties, they increased the amount of surveillance from twelve to sixteen hours per day at very little cost. Without knowing it, the owners applied Jacobs' (1961, p. 50) concept of "constant succession of eyes."

These are small scale examples property owners working together. At the other extreme are Business Improvement Districts (BIDs). BIDs are chartered organizations, based on enabling legislation, that assess businesses in their areas for a fee. In return, they attend to problems of litter, graffiti, other forms of disorder, and sponsor prosocial activities. Often they employ uniformed "hosts" or "ambassadors" who extend the eyes of shopkeepers (Manshel, 2020). We have personally attended numerous meetings of the BID for downtown

Cincinnati and routinely observed how the members and employees organized common spaces, regulated conduct on the streets, and encouraged access to the area. When members identified a business that operated in ways that created trouble, their first efforts were to apply friendly, informal control. This often worked: persuading the manager of a drug store to curb sales of high alcohol beers, for example. If it did not, then the BID would seek help from the city, which brings us to the last way control is exercised.

Control also arises via the small number of financial and governmental institutions who finance and regulate place ownership. As discussed in Section 3, FHA insurance policies encouraged financial institutions to approve mortgages for properties in some areas, but not others (Glotzer, 2020; Jackson, 1985). This impacted who the banks were willing to approve mortgages for. Real estate agents engaged in racial steering and promoted the sale of properties to certain types of people, but not others (Massey & Denton, 1993; Pearce, 1979). These practices impact who the property owners are in any given area. But the property developers we just described do not sit around like Scrooge McDuck on piles of cash. They need financial institutions or government grants and loans to safeguard their money and build wealth.

Even after a person purchases a property and gains control of a place, these financial and governmental entities can further influence the decision-making that he engages in. Sampson et al. (2010) refer to such entities as super controllers. They are "the people, organizations and institutions that create the incentives for controllers to prevent or facilitate crime ... they do not have a direct effect on the necessary conditions for crime, but influence them indirectly through handlers, guardians, and managers" (Sampson et al., 2010, p. 40). For example, an agent regulating alcohol sales does not make any explicit changes to the functioning of a bar, such as serving policies. Instead, she can impose fines on the owner or shut down the bar if the owner does not take adequate action to prevent minors from obtaining alcohol. This provides an economic incentive for owners to make certain management decisions, such as staff training. Therefore, these entities can control larger areas by influencing the decisions of each property owner within that area.

All four sources of control we described demonstrate that control starts at places and extends outward to a wider network. Once place managers create safe and welcoming places, it attracts additional users. This increases the number of people who can act as additional eyes on the street. For those concerned with crime, this means we need to focus our attention on places, their owners, their colleagues, their financiers, and their regulators. We need to understand their decision-making processes and how they are linked to other managers to exert control over wider areas. While most people use these networks to create vibrant safe areas, some create them to carry out illegal activities (Isaac et al., 2017). Much like the 80/20 principle (Koch, 2008), a small number of people control many places. In Section 5, we show the importance of this principle and present a new perspective to guide criminology; a Neo-Jacobian perspective.

5 New Glasses: The Neo-Jacobian Perspective

We provided three turning points for criminology in the last three sections. A turn from residents to place managers, as the primary source of informal social control, is the first. A turn from ecological processes to outsiders' deliberate actions creating crime opportunities is the second. A turn from top-down macrospatial, to a bottom-up microspatial explanation of crime patterns is the third. These turning points encapsulate our Neo-Jacobian perspective. It is a new way of thinking about crime patterns based on the insights of Jane Jacobs. It integrates criminology with its adjacent fields: economics, finance, political science, business, urban planning, and history.

The unifying theme of these turning points is the 80/20 (or Pareto) principle. It states that most outcomes arise from a tiny set of sources: e.g., roughly 80 percent of the results are due to 20 percent of the causes (Koch, 2008). In criminology this is a well-documented phenomenon. Only a few offenders commit most of the offenses (Martinez et al., 2017), a few people experience most of the victimizations (O et al., 2017), and a small percentage of places have most of the crime (Lee et al., 2017). The Neo-Jacobian perspective emphasizes the importance of this principle. A small number of property owners, not a wide array of residents, comprise the primary eyes on the street. Few outsiders own and control a large proportion of the places in urban areas. And few hot places generate most of the crime in city areas. Consequently, we need to focus on the few people and places with the most influence (Martinez et al., 2017; Wilcox & Eck, 2011).

In practice, the three turning points are inseparable: they are braided, one turn prompts the other turns. If city areas are molded by deliberate decisions, we must ask: who makes these decisions? This leads us to consider what these decision-makers gain and leads us to consider property and its value. Property is a microlevel entity; you can own an address, you can own multiple addresses, but you cannot own an entire neighborhood, usually. The concentration of ownership of microplaces implies that a relatively few people control large swaths of cities (Payne, 2010). The connections among owners, real estate interests, financiers, and government planners extends this control. And if a relatively few people or institutions exercise such control, where does this leave residents' informal social control?

As we wrote this, we witnessed an answer to this question. Cincinnati's professional soccer team wanted a new stadium and wanted it built near a vibrant, downtown neighborhood. A poor Black neighborhood on the periphery was ideal for the team's purposes. The team's owners, well-funded and politically connected to the mayor and city council, prevailed over resisting neighborhood residents. This forced some residents and small businesses in the neighborhood to leave. Once built, the stadium will draw thousands of people from outside the area, spurring the growth of new businesses, redevelopment of older housing, and construction of new housing (Coolidge, 2019; Editorial Board, 2017; Swartsell, 2017). It will also change crime patterns. Whether one considers this desirable or not, it is an example of deliberate choices made at a microlevel by nonresident outsiders. As citizens, we can laud or decry such examples. As social scientists, we cannot ignore the reality that for neighborhood change, often residents matter less than do the property owners. As activists, we need to know this in order to achieve social justice. Jane Jacobs knew this. She was a realistic observer of urban processes and a community activist.

As we described the three turning points, we contrasted the dominant community criminology perspective, rooted in an early twentieth-century analogy of cities being ecological, to our Neo-Jacobian perspective, built upon the mid-century works of Jane Jacobs. So far we have written in a tone implying that our perspective should replace the older one. We wrote this way to make our perspective clear; to prevent muddying our points. We will not highlight this contrast further. Instead, we now suggest ways both perspectives could operate simultaneously. These are summarized in the upper portion of Table 1. Later in the section we will discuss the implications for methods and policy shown in the lower portion of Table 1.

Our emphasis on place management, the control of places, and the influence of outsiders, does not rule out residents inside areas exercising informal social control. These insiders could do this whether they own their homes or rent. When the interests of insiders and outsiders coincide, their joint influences could be considerable so social scientists will have difficulty disentangling who controls what. It is when their interests conflict that it is possible to measure who exercises more control. The Neo-Jacobian perspective does not give a single answer. The answers probably vary geographically and historically. But if the residents are poor and have limited political pull, they will lose most of these conflicts. Still, a discerning criminologist can have one foot in each perspective as she uses data to sort things out.

Table 1 The compatibility of perspectives

	COMMUNITY CRIMINOLOGY	NEO-JACOBIAN PERSPECTIVE	ROOM FOR COMPROMISE?
Founding Parent(s)	Robert Park; Ernest Burgess	Jane Jacobs	Not applicable
Disciplinary Foundation	Sociology	Urban planning, economics, citizen activism	Not applicable
Source of Order	Residents	Place managers: those who own and operate places	Yes. Neither perspective rules out the other's source of order. Both may operate. Dominance of a source may vary geographically and historically.
Who Creates the Order	Insiders to neighborhoods: mostly residents	Mix of insiders and outsiders: mostly property owners, but also residents.	Yes. It is possible that both insiders and outsiders contribute to order.
Explanation for High Crime Levels	Residents are unable to create an orderly environment	Politics and economics impede ability of place managers to regulate conduct at their places	Yes. It is possible that some crime is the result of residents' inabilities, and some is the result of poor place management.
Neighborhood	A real entity that naturally emerges from residents shared understanding and interactions	An artifact of bureaucratic and organizational administrative needs. Neighborhoods are not natural.	No

Table 1 (cont.)

	COMMUNITY CRIMINOLOGY	NEO-JACOBIAN PERSPECTIVE	ROOM FOR COMPROMISE?
Research Methods	Surveys and statistical modeling	Experimentation and qualitative observation	Yes. Numerous methods can be applied to provide a richer understanding.
Policies Suggested	Organize residents; Have police impose order	Address incentives for place managers. Government interventions at places on place managers	Yes. In theory both sets of polices could be applied.
Evidence for Policy Effectiveness	Limited	A large number of successful (randomized and quasi) experiments	No. Existing evidence holds little promise for communities and crime interventions across large spatial units but considerable promise for place-based interventions.

Research findings create the lack of compromise over evidence. There is limited evidence community criminology offers useful crime solutions (Gill, 2016). Many studies show place-based interventions do reduce crime (Eck & Guerette, 2012). But new ideas and rigorous experimental research could soften this conclusion. This is not so with the other obstacle to compatibility. The Neo-Jacobian perspective rejects the idea that neighborhoods are natural. The term neighborhood is relevant to those engaged in property markets. They use neighborhood labels to signal the value of their properties. Institutions set the boundaries of labeled neighborhoods for their own needs: e.g., delivering mail, counting residents, enrolling students in schools. A community criminology perspective can be compatible with the Neo-Jacobian perspective if its adherents abandon the notion of the natural neighborhood. Weisburd and colleagues (2012, 2021b) have shown how they can do this: adopt the street segment as a unit of analysis. They have defined this unit rigorously and can operationalize it consistently. They provide a sound mechanism; if locals' interactions are the foundation of informal control, then residents are more likely to interact on a street segment. Street segments are highly compatible with the Neo-Jacobian perspective.

Adherence to the dominant ecological perspective created a "criminological blind spot" (Unnever et al., 2009, p. 396). It kept criminologists from seeing key arguments in Jacobs' work. It has kept criminologists from asking questions that need asking, investigating topics that need investigation, and exploring policies that need exploring. Our field would advance further if criminologists informed their inquiries with multiple perspectives. The Neo-Jacobian perspective brings into the realm of criminological inquiry a range of actors and processes that up to now have been on the periphery of criminological interest. In particular, it requires criminologists to take on the purposeful creation of cities by elites. Below we detail what the Neo-Jacobian perspective has to offer to criminology as well as its methodological and policy implications.

THE NEO-JACOBIAN PERSPECTIVE

The three turning points we described define the core of the Neo-Jacobian perspective on crime. We should pay close attention to those who own and control property and the processes that occur on those properties. Their choices strongly influence the volume of crime at places. Their influence on misbehavior percolates outward onto streets but declines with distance from their properties. Those who own and operate properties may live far from their properties; many are outsiders. They form place management networks that include supporting institutions: financial, regulatory, marketing, and others. Therefore, outsiders can exercise considerable control over misbehavior in an area. The Barksdale Market example illustrates this point; the owner lived in another state. The more economically and politically depressed an area, the greater the likelihood that relative control swings to outsiders compared to insiders. Further, there is a greater chance that the outsiders have limited connections to and empathy with insiders.

Jacobs' examples we have provided point to the importance of action occurring at specific microspatial places by their proprietors and managers. Her ideas point to a bottom-up approach to understanding neighborhood crime. Tangible microgeographic units (property parcels and street segments) and documentable powers of control (deeds, leases, contracts, agreements, regulations, laws, and court decisions) ground this perspective. We can easily identify the spatial boundaries of proprietary places, their owners, their users, and government restrictions. We can also trace the government, business, and lending policies that influence decision-making processes at these places. The place – property parcel, business, or street segment – is the building block.

Consequently, our perspective tells us to pay attention to two core principles. First, place functioning is the foundation for understanding crime in larger areas. Some of the crime observed at larger units of analysis is just the sum of crime occurring at microspatial places (Eck, 2019; Linning, 2019). Some of the crime in larger areas only occurs because of the opportunity structures created at nearby places (e.g., robberies of patrons walking from a bar to a parking area). And some of the crime in larger areas come from nonplace processes, but for which networks of places form a context. This can be summarized as: $Ct = Cp + Cd + Co + Cr$, where Ct is the total crime in an area, Cp is crime occurring at a place, Cd is crime diffused from a place to its surroundings, Co is crime from other processes (including ecological ones), and Cr is random crime. Cp and Cd are the subject of the Neo-Jacobian Perspective. Co and Cr are not.

Although no theory can explain Cr, theories based in a human ecology perspective could explain Co. The simple additive equation we offer, provides one way of integrating human ecology of resident theories with theories based on a Neo-Jacobian perspective. Another way to integrate these two perspective is to view them as alternative foregrounds and backgrounds. From a Neo-Jacobian perspective, community processes are part of a backcloth: outside investors may choose where to place their money, and place managers may choose their practices, based on their perceptions of human ecology. From a community criminology perspective, Neo-Jacobian processes are part of the backcloth.

Second, deliberate choices of property owners, government agents, and private decision-makers influence many of the crime opportunities. Owners acquire properties for a reason, often for economic gain. In doing so, they receive the legal powers to control them. This includes deciding what the property will be used for and dictating what behaviors they will allow by those who use it (Eck, 1994, 2018). Deliberate choices about places influences activity at these places. The activities may be intentional and unintentional. Crime is one such activity and is often unintentional (Linning & Eck, 2018). What owners do with their properties will have some influence on crime. It will either suppress or encourage crime (Eck & Madensen, 2018). Economics drives most of their choices. They want to attract customers to generate profits. We must look to the incentives that place managers have for their properties. These can come from the costs of owning, maintaining, and operating their properties as well as government tax, regulatory, and subsidy schemes, and markets for the property and whatever goods or services the property produces.

In essence, the Neo-Jacobian perspective extends place management theory to explain variations in crime across larger areas (Eck, 1994; Eck & Madensen, 2018). While addresses and property parcels remain the fundamental unit of analysis, it shows how control radiates out to wider areas. Moreover, while the owners and operators of places are still the primary actors to focus on, the Neo-Jacobian perspective reveals additional actors with influence. Government agents and institutions that influence owners – such as real estate agents, banks, and insurance companies – can influence decision-making at places. Doing this across multiple properties can permit agents to impose control over larger areas. Much control across larger areas is based on control of individual properties within the area or networks of property owners that transcend neighborhood boundaries. Consequently, our best methodological and policy practices should focus on identifying and understanding the few who can invoke the greatest change.

IMPLICATIONS FOR METHODS

The Neo-Jacobian perspective suggests that we need to be hyper-focused. A few places and a few owners can exert much control across cities. Much of this depends on economic and political processes. Criminological studies need to account for this. It requires a shift from large-scale surveys using "residents as informants about neighborhood context" (Sampson, 2002, p. 218), to focusing on those who can exert control over places and across areas. This can include anyone from property owners to city planners, government officials, and banking agents. Residents can play a role, and should be included, but they should not be the only focus of our studies. In fact, Jacobs points out that it is often only a small number of exceptional residents who can influence any larger-level processes. She should know; Jacobs was one of these exceptional community members who often fought against change by elites in New York City (Flint, 2011; Kanigel, 2016).

We are unlikely to capture exceptional residents in probability surveys of all residents. This may be another example of concentration: even among residents, most power is concentrated in a few, and most residents exert little power. To researchers, the opinions of a few exceptional residents will appear to be outliers. Worse, such surveys will not capture the point of view of powerful people who live outside the neighborhood. Thus, criminologists need to devise ways to study these small groups of people and their powers.

We should also be conducting far more fieldwork. Jacobs was a proponent of conducting extensive fieldwork to understand the places she was studying. As Kanigel (2016, p. 176) states:

> *The Death and Life of Great American Cities* could seem so much the product of Jane's distinctive intellect that one might forget that it was "researched": she visited cities, talked to people, traded ideas with experts, gathered statistics, sought out pointed bits of knowledge.

Examples in Jacobs' (1961) seminal book feature cities such as New York, Toronto, Boston, Philadelphia, Cincinnati, and Pittsburgh, among others. Some of her earlier work covers city-building practices in Cleveland, Washington, Fort Worth, and Baltimore (Zipp & Storring, 2017). In fact, she spent much of 1955 researching renewal efforts in Philadelphia and toured the city with planning officials (Jacobs, 1955). She did not conduct large-scale surveys and she did not download someone else's dataset for secondary analysis. She visited the locations of which she spoke, and she spoke to the people who controlled those locations.

Taking a Neo-Jacobian perspective seriously requires methods different from those typically used to study neighborhoods. Neo-Jacobian research demands case studies and mixed methods research. Doing so will increase our ability to identify potential causal mechanisms that are operating in city areas. As Jacobs argues, we need to interact far more with the people and places we study. Oftentimes, it generates a wealth of new insights and ideas. As she puts it:

> You've got to get out and walk. Walk, and you will see that many of the assumptions on which projects depend are visibly wrong .... If you get out and walk, you see all sorts of other clues. Why is the hub of downtown such a mixture of things? Why do office workers on New York's handsome Park Avenue turn off to Lexington or Madison Avenue at the first corner they reach? Why is a good steak house usually in an old building? Why are short blocks apt to be busier than long ones? (Jacobs, 1958, p. 142)

In criminology, this requires extensive fieldwork to understand the large-scale quantitative datasets we analyze. When we identify a crime hot spot, what does it look like? Why is it hot? Who uses it? How do they use it? What are the police doing to address crime there? What is the place manager doing (or failing to do) to control it? Are nearby residents involved? We cannot answer these questions unless we heed Jacobs' advice and get out and walk.

Quantitative work on places and neighborhoods should continue, but such work will be unhelpful if criminologists fail to address ownership. Just asking if respondents rent or own barely touches the subject. Criminologists should also consider the concentration of ownership (Lee et al., 2021). Do a small number of people own multiple properties in a given area? Similarly, we should consider the prevalence of absentee ownership. Some property owners live in other cities, states, or even countries entirely. We should endeavor to locate parcel-level characteristics that may influence crime processes both at the place and at a larger scale. We should embrace studies that integrate a variety of qualitative and quantitative methodologies to show how people and places connect to protect against crime. Details matter, and they matter most to inform better policies.

Lastly, criminologists must consider history. History goes back more than a decade or two, so panel studies are not the answer. Historians, urban planners, and others have provided a wealth of evidence from history that informs how cities are created and change. Sensitivity to history not only broadens our understanding of the long-term consequences of distant acts, it tells us who is acting. Unlike ecological studies of neighborhood crime, historical studies give names – individuals and institutions – and provide reasons. Recent work by the Federal Reserve Bank of Chicago shows that 1930's policy choices to exclude Black neighborhoods from federal loan guarantees continue to shape neighborhoods today (Aaronson et al., 2017). Understanding the prevalence of historic racial restrictions (Nelson et al., 2020) in a neighborhood may predict current levels of ethnic heterogeneity as well as population mobility. Although we reviewed historical evidence of these practices in the United States, deliberate action – such as urban renewal programs – has been used in countries all over the world, including Canada, Britain, Germany, France, the Netherlands, and China (Aalbers, 2006; Adams & Hastings, 2001; Couch et al., 2011; Klemek, 2011; Pickett, 1968).

In addition to the nationally observed history found in government legislation, real estate, and lending practices, each neighborhood has its own local history too. We can better understand our study areas, if we examine them like Jacobs did. Her extensive use of examples came from spending countless hours walking the streets of the places she wrote about and speaking with people directly involved in their functioning (Jacobs, 1961; Kanigel, 2016). Our fieldwork, interviews, and study of history in Walnut Hills gave us a much stronger understanding of the crime trends we observed. The stories our participants shared, and the redevelopment we witnessed, helped us understand the quantitative crime patterns that would have otherwise seemed anomalous (Linning, 2019).

POLICY IMPLICATIONS

The Neo-Jacobian perspective also implies that some policing strategies to control crime are naïve. Consider two strategies, often considered antithetical, with roots in the community criminology perspective: community policing and broken windows policing. Advocates for either will find little comfort in our perspective if they expect their strategies to reduce crime. The Neo-Jacobian perspective suggests that controls over behavior are in large part due to property owners, many of whom are not residents in the community. Some do not even care about the area. Indeed, the Neo-Jacobian perspective helps explain why such organizing is the least effective in areas that need it most: poor, high crime areas. For residents of these areas to have an impact on crime, they need to be able to exert pressure on property owners whose activities facilitate crime. Not only do these property owners typically live elsewhere, often they have more economic, legal, and political clout than residents. Police efforts to assist residents will be constrained by limits on their own powers, particularly when owners have strong networks with elected officials. There may be many reasons to have community policing (Gill et al., 2014), but producing a direct and sustainable impact on crime and disorder is among the least of these reasons.

Wilson and Kelling (1982) built their broken windows theory on a human ecology foundation. They suggest that residents exert control over behaviors. Informal social control breaks down as areas go into decline created by increasing disorder and fear. To reestablish residents' control, police should suppress disorder, which reduces fear and crime, which encourages residents to reemerge and work together. The metaphor is the "broken window." Yet, renters have little control over the integrity of real or metaphorical windows.

Hot spots policing has the same basic problem. Unlike community and broken windows policing, there is strong and consistent evidence that it does suppress disorder and can reduce crime (Braga et al., 2019). But this effect is short lived (Sherman, 1990), so disorder and crime return once police move on to other pressing problems. Without a way of controlling property, hot spots policing is not a long-term strategy, but a short-term tactic best used with strategies that can create lasting change. Improvements in predicting hot spots cannot overcome this limitation.

Community policing in combination with a rigorous application of problem-oriented policing is the best police can do. Problem-oriented policing can deliver crime reductions over modest time periods (Hinkle et al., 2020). One reason is that problem-oriented police often do pay attention to who owns what and how owners' actions influence public safety (Eck, 2014). Police, using this strategy, can compel some owners to do better. With problem-oriented policing addressing public safety, community policing can assure that police are aware of residents' concerns and help craft solutions that have the least negative consequences for residents. A tenacious community-orientation is essential to prevent police from becoming the handmaiden of gentrification.

Two principles draw the boundary between useful policing in the public interest and policing for property developers. The first is the intent; would police address a problem property in the absence of interest from developers? The second is harm (Ratcliffe, 2015); is the place a serious threat to public safety? If the Barksdale had fostered a peaceful illicit marijuana trade, and had been seized to further redevelopment, then the city would have been promoting the interests of developers over the interests of many residents. We advocate for community policing along with a problem-oriented approach to help police navigate this boundary.

The Neo-Jacobian perspective also points to a set of crime prevention strategies that do not require police involvement. Property owners often do not realize how much power they have (Linning, 2019). Their decision-making processes impact the presence or absence of crime opportunities. Many property developers are interested in knowing how to keep crime at bay. After all, this typically leads to increased property values. The problem is that they often do not know what to do or how. Oftentimes, this simply stems from unawareness. As Peiser (1997) notes,

> Real estate owners and developers have considerable experience in dealing with different types of crime . . .. The fact that the major real estate organizations and companies have little awareness of Crime Prevention Through Environmental Design (CPTED) research points to the principle problem – lack of communication between the real estate community and criminologists . . .. If criminologists want to have an impact, they will have to find ways to capture the attention of property owners. Surely, the best way to do that is to provide solutions that save property owners money. In the long run, the dialogue should not only save property owners money, but should help to save entire neighborhoods – to stop the ever-quickening cycle of real

estate investment, deterioration, property disinvestment and neighborhood abandonment that plagues American cities. (Peiser, 1997, p. 232)

This call to criminologists is certainly no small feat. It requires both intensive research on our part to explore the many possible ways place managers can prevent crime as well as disseminating that information to those who have the power to enact our suggestions. If we can show the benefits of crime prevention to owners, especially the economic ones, we will be more likely to convince them to invest in certain practices. Similar to what Newman (1973) argued, many crime-reducing decisions can be made at little cost to owners. The trick is to inform them of what these optimal decisions are.

An example of a nonpolice involved crime prevention effort stems from Jacobs' idea of diversity of land use to increase the number of eyes on the street. Variation in types of places can come from careful planning by private investors or government agencies. Property developers possess the power to decide who to lease their properties to. Implementing this mixture of places strategy could be very beneficial to cities (Linning, 2019). Similarly, community development corporations can influence the purchase of properties that have gone into receivership and need a new owner (Mallach, 2006). Local governments can influence operations of properties by imposing regulations through building and business permits (Eck & Eck, 2012).

Lastly, we need a better understanding of how to intervene when poor place management is taking place. Jacobs' (1961, p. 36) suggestion to vary the types of places "sprinkled along the sidewalks" implies that we want places run by responsible managers who suppress crime. In reality, we know this is not always the case. One of the most effective ways to encourage responsible management is to extend our knowledge of how super controllers can invoke desired behavior from property owners (Sampson et al., 2010). Different actors have formal, diffuse, or personal powers that can pressure those with property rights to act in crime suppressing ways. Personal and group super controllers could be residents. But similar to the frequency with which Jacobs discusses the power of residents in achieving neighborhood order, Sampson et al.'s (2010) typologies suggest that they make up a small proportion of super controllers.

We can supplement problem-solving efforts by engaging with the formal and diffuse super controllers who can leverage action from place managers. This might include creating chronic nuisance ordinances for properties that generate a disproportionate number of police calls for service (Mazerolle & Roehl, 1998). It could involve creating vacant property receivership legislation to force owners to rehabilitate vacant buildings or risk losing them altogether

(Kelly Jr., 2004). We could also compel corporate businesses to change shop-lifting policies to address disproportionate amounts of crime being generated at single store locations (Zidar et al., 2018). Municipalities can also enact policies that encourage responsible place management practices and discourage undesir-able ones. To achieve the former, cities can provide tax abatements, forgiveness of liens, or landlord training to encourage responsible owners to take over properties (Mallach, 2006; Reno et al., 2000). Conversely, they can implement differential property tax rates, fees, or liens against properties that generate problems such as calls for police or fire services or rodent infestations that compromise the health of persons in neighboring properties (Mallach, 2006).

The Neo-Jacobian perspective points to other local government policies. At the beginning of this section, we gave a recent example of government facilitating the destruction of a neighborhood for a sports stadium. The scale of such destruction is small, compared to urban renewal projects of the 1950s, but they are not trivial. The crime impacts of such projects cannot be over-looked. Some might suppress crime, but others might create crime facilitating conditions at the site or further afield where displaced renters are forced to settle. Crime is the byproduct of decisions and actions made for reasons seemingly unconnected with crime. Indeed, this is the core lesson of routine activities theory (Cohen & Felson, 1979), and environmental criminology in general. If criminologists channel their efforts into learning about these experiences and disseminate them to wide audiences, we can help property developers, city officials, and business owners make more informed decisions that create safer city areas.

6 Conclusion

We wrote this Element to prompt criminologists to ask new questions. Faced with a neighborhood we could not understand using the existing perspectives, we turned to Jane Jacobs' work, which led us to other fields. When we looked at Walnut Hills up close, we had to contend with a few outsiders and their places. Once we knew the history of the area, crime patterns made more sense. Once responsible place managers took ownership of places like the Barksdale Market, crime problems declined widely. With the growth of a prosocial network of property owners in Walnut Hills, crime reduction effects were sustained. This was very different from what we read in traditional criminology. Residents played a much smaller role in these changes than that literature suggests. Shaw and McKay's (1942) social disorganization theory did not explain what was going on. Kornhauser's (1978) neighborhood control model did not fit. Wilson and Kelling's (1982) broken windows thesis could not account for what was happening. Sampson et al.'s (1997) resident-focused, collective efficacy theory was not evident. Hot spot patrol strategies had little long run impact.

Criminology's standard explanations direct us to particular questions and methods. The human ecology perspective of the 1920s continues to dominate our thinking: Why are some communities unable "to realize the common values of their residents or solve commonly experienced problems" (Bursik, 1988, p. 521; Kornhauser, 1978)? Are there "informal mechanisms by which residents themselves achieve public order" (Sampson et al., 1997, p. 918)? "How can the police strengthen the informal social-control mechanisms of natural communities in order to minimize fear in public places" (Wilson & Kelling, 1982, p. 81)?

In light of the evidence we have presented, it is time for criminologists to begin asking new questions. At the risk of being glib, what questions would Jane Jacobs ask? We imagine her asking, "Have you looked for yourself?" She would have walked the streets watching who uses them and how. She would have looked to see which buildings were in active use, their condition, who was using them, and what they were being used for. She would have noticed a building causing most of the trouble and asked: "Who owns that building with the broken window? Why haven't they fixed it?"

References

Aalbers, M.B. (2006). "When the banks withdraw, slum lords take over": The structuration of neighborhood decline through redlining, drug dealing, speculation and immigrant exploitation. *Urban Studies, 43*(7), 1061–86.

Aaronson, D., Hartley, D., & Mazumder, B. (2017). *The effects of the 1930s HOLC "redlining" maps.* Chicago, IL: Federal Reserve Bank of Chicago.

Abrams, C. (1955). *Forbidden neighbors: A study in prejudice in housing.* Port Washington, NY: Kennikat Press.

Adams, D. & Hastings, E.M. (2001). Urban renewal in Hong Kong: Transition from development corporation to renewal authority. *Land Use Policy, 18*, 245–58.

Anaheim Police Department. (2007). The Boogie! A nightclub that defied traditional problem solving efforts. Finalist for 1995 Goldstein Award for Excellence in Problem-Oriented Policing. https://popcenter.asu.edu/sites/default/files/library/awards/goldstein/2007/07-01(F).pdf

Antero, P. (2010). *Not in my neighborhood: How bigotry shaped a great American city.* Chicago, IL: Ivan R. Dee Publishers.

Borrion, H. & Koch, D. (2019). Architecture. In R. Wortley, A. Sidebottom, N. Tilley, & G. Laycock (eds.), *Routledge handbook of crime science* (pp. 145–66). New York: Routledge.

Bowers, K. (2014). Risky facilities: Crime radiators or crime absorbers? A comparison of internal and external levels of theft. *Journal of Quantitative Criminology, 30*(3), 389–414.

Bowers, K. & Johnson, S.D. (2017). Burglary prevention in practice. In N. Tilley & A. Sidebottom (eds.), *Handbook of crime prevention and community safety*, 2nd ed. (pp. 319–53). New York: Routledge.

Bowers, K.J., Johnson, S.D., Guerette, R.T., Summers, L., & Poynton, S. (2011). Spatial displacement and diffusion of benefits among geographically focused policing initiatives: A meta-analytical review. *Journal of Experimental Criminology, 7*(4), 347–74.

Braga, A.A., Turchan, B.S., Papachristos, A.V., & Hureau, D.M. (2019). Hot spots policing and crime reduction: An update of an ongoing systematic review and meta-analysis. *Journal of Experimental Criminology, 15*(3), 289–311.

Brantingham, P.L. & Brantingham, P.J. (1995). Criminality of place. *European Journal on Criminal Policy and Research, 3*(3), 5–26.

Brantingham, P.L. & Brantingham, P.J. (1993). Nodes, paths and edges: Considerations on the complexity of crime and the physical environment. *Journal of Environmental Psychology, 13*(1), 3–28.

Browning, C.R., Byron, R.A., Calder, C.A., Krivo, L.J., Kwan, M., Lee, J., & Peterson, R.D. (2010). Commercial density, residential concentration, and crime: Land use patterns and violence in neighborhood context. *Journal of Research in Crime and Delinquency, 47*(3), 329–57.

Browning, C.R., Calder, C.A., Boettner, B., & Smith, A. (2017a). Ecological networks and urban crime: The structure of shared routine activity locations and neighborhood-level informal control capacity. *Criminology, 55*(4), 754–78.

Browning, C.R., Calder, C.A., Soller, B., Jackson, A.L., & Dirlam, J. (2017b). Ecological networks and neighborhood social organization. *American Journal of Sociology, 122*(6), 1939–88.

Buchanan & Warley, 245 U.S. 60 (1917).

Bursik, R.J. (1988). Social disorganization and theories of crime and delinquency: Problems and prospects. *Criminology, 26*(4), 519–51.

Bursik, R.J. & Grasmick, H. (1993). *Neighborhoods and crime: The dimensions of effective social control*. New York: Lexington.

Caro, R. (1974). *The power broker: Robert Moses and the fall of New York*. New York: Alfred A. Knopf Inc.

Clark, T.C. & Perlman, P.B. (1948). *Prejudice and property: An historic brief against racial covenants*. Washington, DC: Public Affairs Press.

Clarke, R.V. (1995). Situational crime prevention. *Crime and Justice, 19*, 91–150.

Clarke, R.V. & Weisburd, D. (1994). Diffusion of crime control benefits: Observations on the reverse of displacement. *Crime Prevention Studies, 2*, 165–84.

Cohen, L.E. & Felson, M. (1979). Social change and crime rate trends: A routine activity approach. *American Sociological Review, 44*(4), 588–608.

Coolidge, S. (2019, April 25). Berding: Council's demands "outside the law," but he's working with displaced tenants. *Cincinnati Enquirer*. www.cincin nati.com/story/sports/soccer/fc-cincinnati/2019/04/25/berding-councils-fc-cincinnati-stadium-ultimatum/3572539002/

Copsey, H. (2018, February). Are city neighborhoods "beating" The Banks? Some say yes, but The Banks is a neighborhood, too. *WCPO News*. www .wcpo.com/news/insider/are-city-neighborhoods-beating-the-banks-some-say-yes-but-the-banks-is-a-neighborhood-too

Couch, C., Sykes, O., & Borstinghaus, W. (2011). Thirty years of urban regeneration in Britain, Germany, and France: The importance of context and path dependency. *Progress in Planning, 75*, 1–52.

Cozens, P. (2008). Crime prevention through environmental design. In R. Wortley & L. Mazerolle (eds.), *Environmental criminology and crime analysis*, 1st ed. (pp. 153–77). New York: Routledge.

Cozens, P. & Hillier, D. (2012). Revisiting Jane Jacob's "eyes on the street" for the twenty-first century: Evidence from environmental criminology. In S. Hart & D. Zahm (eds.), *The urban wisdom of Jane Jacobs* (pp. 196–214). New York: Routledge.

de Wolfe, I. (1963, February). The death and life of great American citizens. *The Architectural Review, 133*(792), 90–3.

Demeropolis, T. (2019, February). Three retail tenants coming to Paramount Square in Walnut Hills. *Cincinnati Business Courier*. www.bizjournals.com/cincinnati/news/2019/02/07/exclusive-three-retail-tenants-coming-to-paramount.html

Dorsey v. Stuyvesant Town Corporation, 299 N.Y. 2d 541 (N.Y. App. 2d 1949).

Douglas, S. & Welsh, B.C. (2020). Place managers for crime prevention: The theoretical and empirical status of a neglected situational crime prevention technique. *Crime Prevention and Community Safety, 22*, 99–109.

Duneier, M. (1999). *Sidewalk*. New York: Farrar, Straus and Giroux.

Eck, J.E. (2019). Race, place management, and crime. In J.D. Unnever, S. L. Gabbidon, & C. Chouhy (eds.), *Building a Black criminology: Race, theory, and crime* (pp. 171–206). New York: Routledge.

Eck, J.E. (2018). The opportunity structure for bad place management: A theory to assist effective regulation of high crime places. In D. Weisburd & J.E. Eck (eds.), *Unraveling the crime-place connection: New directions in theory and policy* (pp. 157–87). New York: Routledge.

Eck, J.E. (2014). There is nothing so theoretical as good practice: Police-researcher coproduction of place theory. In J. Knutsson & E. Cockbain (eds.), *Applied police research: Challenges and opportunities* (pp. 129–40). London: Routledge.

Eck, J.E. (1997). Do premise liability suits promote business crime prevention? In R.V. Clarke & M. Felson (eds.), *Business and crime prevention* (pp. 125–50). Monsey, NY: Criminal Justice Press.

Eck, J.E. (1994). Drug markets and drug places: A case-control study of the spatial structure of illicit drug dealing. Unpublished doctoral dissertation, University of Maryland College Park.

Eck, J.E. & Eck, E.B. (2012). Crime place and pollution: Expanding crime reduction options through a regulatory approach. *Criminology & Public Policy, 11*(2), 281–316.

Eck, J.E. & Guerette, R.T. (2012). Place-based crime prevention: Theory, evidence, and policy. In B. Welsh & D. Farrington (eds.), *The Oxford Handbook of Crime Prevention* (pp. 354–83). New York: Oxford University Press.

Eck, J.E. & Linning, S.J. (2019). Hidden in plain sight: What criminologists should know and teach but do not. *The Criminologist, 44*(4), 1–7.

Eck, J.E. & Madensen, T.D. (2018). Place management. In G.J.N. Bruinsma & S.D. Johnson (eds.), *The Oxford handbook of environmental criminology* (pp. 629–63). New York: Oxford University Press.

Editorial Board. (2017, November 29). FC Cincinnati stadium debate insulted the people who matter – The public. WCPO. www.wcpo.com/news/opinion/editorial-fc-cincinnati-stadium-debate-insulted-the-people-who-matter-the-public

Edmonton Police Service. (1995). The Klondiker hotel project: Hotels, crime, and problem-solving on the beat. Finalist for 1995 Goldstein Award for Excellence in Problem-Oriented Policing. https://popcenter.asu.edu/sites/default/files/library/awards/goldstein/1995/95-21(F).pdf

Felson, M. (1995). Those who discourage crime. In J.E. Eck & D. Weisburd (eds.), *Crime and place*, Vol. 4 (pp. 53–66). Monsey, NY: Criminal Justice Press.

FHA Underwriting Manual. (1936). *Underwriting manual: Underwriting and valuation procedure under Title II of the National Housing Act*. Washington, DC: Federal Housing Administration.

Fischel, W.A. (2004). An economic history of zoning and a cure for its exclusionary effects. *Urban Studies, 41*(2), 317–40.

Flint, A. (2011). *Wrestling with Moses: How Jane Jacobs took on New York's master builder and transformed the American city*. New York: Random House.

Freund, D.M. (2007). *Colored property: State policy and white racial politics in suburban America*. Chicago, IL: University of Chicago Press.

Gans, H.J. (1962, February). City planning and urban realities. *Culture & Civilization, 33*(2), 170–5.

Gelfand, M.I. (1975). *A nation of cities: The federal government in urban America, 1933–1965*. New York: Oxford University Press.

Gerard, D.W. (2016). A look at an offender-based crime strategy. Presented at the University of Cincinnati on March 7, 2016.

Ghosh, S., Silveria, J., & Erickson, T. (2009). *Walnut Hills: An analysis of current conditions*. Structure and dynamics of human settlements. www.uc.edu/cdc/urban_database/subregional/walnut_hills_analysis.pdf

Giglierano, G.J., Overmyer, D.A., & Propas, F.L. (1988). *The bicentennial guide to greater Cincinnati: A portrait of two hundred years*. Cincinnati, OH: The Cincinnati Historical Society.

Gill, C. (2016). Community interventions. In D. Weisburd, D.P. Farrington, & C. Gill (eds.), *What works in crime prevention and rehabilitation* (pp. 77–109). New York: Springer.

Gill, C., Weisburd, D., Telep, C.W., Vitter, Z., & Bennett, T. (2014). Community-oriented policing to reduce crime, disorder and fear and increase satisfaction and legitimacy among citizens: A systematic review. *Journal of Experimental Criminology, 10*(4), 399–428.

Gillette Jr., H. (1999). Assessing James Rouse's role in American city planning. *Journal of the American Planning Association, 65*(2), 151–67.

Glotzer, P. (2020). *How the suburbs were segregated: Developers and the business of exclusionary housing, 1890–1960*. New York: Columbia University Press.

Gotham, K.F. (2002). Beyond invasion and succession: school segregation, real estate blockbusting, and the political economy of neighborhood racial transition. *City & Community, 1*(1), 83–111.

Gotham, K.F. (2000). Urban space, restrictive covenants and the origins of racial residential segregation in a US city, 1900–50. *International Journal of Urban and Regional Research, 24*(3), 616–33.

Groff, E. (2015). Informal social control and crime events. *Journal of Contemporary Criminal Justice, 31*(1), 90–106.

Groner, I.N. & Helfeld, D.M. (1948). Race discrimination in housing. The *Yale Law Journal, 57*(3), 426–58.

Guerette, R.T. & Bowers, K. (2009). Assessing the extent of crime displacement and diffusion of benefits: A review of situational crime prevention evaluations. *Criminology, 47*(4), 1331–68.

Harris, R. (2011). The magpie and the bee: Jane Jacobs's magnificent obsession. In M. Page & T. Minnel (eds.), *Reconsidering Jane Jacobs* (pp. 65–84). Chicago, IL: American Planning Association.

Harriss, C.L. (1951). History and policies of the Home Owners' Loan Corporation. Cambridge, MA: National Bureau of Economic Research.

Helper, R. (1969). *Racial policies and practices of real estate brokers*. Minneapolis, MN: University of Minnesota Press.

Henderson, A.S. (2000). *Housing and the democratic idea: The life and thought of Charles Abrams*. New York: Columbia University Press.

Hill, C.D. (1983). Epilogue. In C.D. Hill (ed.), *Walnut Hills city neighborhood* (The Neighborhood Studies Project of the Cincinnati Historical Society), (pp. 38–45). Cincinnati, OH: Cincinnati Historical Society.

Hillier, A.E. (2003). Redlining and the Home Owners' Loan Corporation. *Journal of Urban History, 29*(4), 394–420.

Hillier, B. (2004). Can streets be made safe? *Urban Design International, 9*(1), 31–45.

Hinkle, J.C., Weisburd, D., Telep, C.W., & Petersen, K. (2020). Problem-oriented policing for reducing crime and disorder: An updated systematic review and meta-analysis. *Campbell Systematic Reviews, 16*(2). DOI: 10.1002/c12.1089

Hipp, J.R. (2010). Resident perceptions of crime and disorder: How much is "bias," and how much is social environment differences? *Criminology, 48*(2), 475–508.

Hipp, J.R. & Boessen, A. (2013). Egohoods as waves washing across the city: A new measure of "neighborhoods." *Criminology, 51*(2), 287–327.

Hope, T. (1995). Community crime prevention. In M. Tonry & D.P. Farrington (eds.), *Building a safer society: Strategic approaches to crime prevention* (pp. 21–90). Chicago, IL: University of Chicago Press.

Hoppenfeld, M. (1962). Review: The death and life of great American cities. *Journal of the American Institute of Planners, 28*, 136–7.

Hoyt, H. (1963). The forces underlying city growth and structure. In H. Hoyt, *According to Hoyt: 53 years of Homer Hoyt, 1916 to 1969* (pp. 296–305). Washington, DC: Homer Hoyt.

Hoyt, H. (1939). *Structure and growth of residential neighborhoods in American cities*. Washington, DC: Federal Housing Administration.

Hoyt, H. (1933). *One hundred years of land values in Chicago*. Chicago, IL: University of Chicago Press.

Hurley, D. (2006). Kenyon Barr Collection: Cincinnati Historical Society Library. *Ohio Valley History, 6*(1), 61–4. http://rave.ohiolink.edu/ejournals/article/320695401

Isaac, E., Hammer, M.G., Christenson, B.R., & Madensen, T. (2017). *Place-based investigations of violent offender territories* (P.I.V.O.T.). Goldstein Award Winner. https://popcenter.asu.edu/sites/default/files/17-15.pdf

Jackson, K.T. (1985). *Crabgrass frontier: The suburbanization of the United States*. New York: Oxford University Press.

Jacobs, J. (2000). *The nature of economies*. New York: Vintage.

Jacobs, J. (1985). *Cities and the wealth of nations: Principles of economic life*. New York: Vintage.

Jacobs, J. (1981). Can big plans solve the problem of renewal? In S. Zipp & N. Storring (eds.), *Vital little plans: The short works of Jane Jacobs* (pp. 177–88). New York: Random House.

Jacobs, J. (1969). *The economy of cities*. New York: Vintage.

Jacobs, J. (1961). *The death and life of great American cities*. New York: Vintage.

Jacobs, J. (1958). Downtown is for people. In W.H. Whyte Jr. (ed.), *The exploding metropolis* (pp. 140–68). New York: Doubleday.

Jacobs, J. (1956, June). The missing link in city redevelopment. *Architectural Forum: The Magazine of Building, 104*(6), 132–3.

Jacobs, J. (1955, July). Philadelphia's redevelopment: A progress report (First appearance in *Architectural Forum*). In S. Zipp & N. Storring (eds.), *Vital *little plans: The short works of Jane Jacobs* (pp. 44–51). New York: Random House.

John, M. (2020, July 27). Newly renovated condo complex in Walnut Hills once housed Black travelers during segregation. WCPO 9 Cincinnati. www.wcpo .com/news/transportation-development/move-up-cincinnati/newly-redeveloped-condo-complex-in-walnut-hills-once-housed-black-travelers-during-segregation

Jones-Correa, M. (2000). The origins and diffusion of racial restrictive covenants. *Political Science Quarterly, 115*(4), 541–68.

Kanigel, R. (2016). *Eyes on the street: The life of Jane Jacobs*. New York: Penguin Random House LLC.

Kelly Jr., J.J. (2004). Refreshing the heart of the city: Vacant building receivership as a tool for neighborhood revitalization and community empowerment. *Journal of Affordable Housing, 13*(2), 210–38.

Kimble, J. (2007). Insuring inequality: The role of the Federal Housing Administration in the urban ghettoization of African Americans. *Law & Social Inquiry, 32*(2), 399–434.

Klemek, C. (2011). *The transatlantic collapse of urban renewal: Postwar urbanism from New York to Berlin*. Chicago, IL: University of Chicago Press.

Klemek, C. (2008). From political outsider to power broker in two "Great American Cities": Jane Jacobs and the fall of the urban renewal order in New York and Toronto. *Journal of Urban History, 34*(2), 309–32.

Koch, R. (2008). *The 80/20 principle: The secret of achieving more with less*. New York: Doubleday.

Konermann, A. (2017, February 10). 25,737 people lived in Kenyon-Barr when the city razed it to the ground. *Cincinnati Magazine*. www.cincinnatimagazine.com /citywiseblog/lost-city-kenyon-barr-queensgate/

Kornhauser, R.R. (1978). *Social sources of delinquency: An appraisal of analytic models*. Chicago, IL: University of Chicago Press.

Kuklick, H. (1980). Chicago sociology and urban planning policy. *Theory and Society, 89*(6), 821–45.

Lee, Y., Eck, J.E., O, S., & Martinez, N.N. (2017). How concentrated is crime at places? A systematic review from 1970 to 2015. *Crime Science, 6*(1), 6.

Lee, Y., O, S., & Eck, J.E. (2021). Why your bar has crime but not mine: Resolving the land use and crime – risky facility conflict. *Justice Quarterly*, DOI: https://doi.org/10.1080/07418825.2021.1903068

Leisch, J.P. (1993). Freeway and interchange design: A historical perspective. *Transportation Research Record No. 1385; Intersection and Interchange Design* (pp. 60–68). Washington, DC: National Academy Press.

Light, J.S. (2009). *The nature of cities: Ecological visions and the American urban professions, 1920–1960*. Baltimore, MD: Johns Hopkins University Press.

Linning, S.J. (2019). The Neo-Jacobian perspective of place and neighborhood crime: A case study of property management, redevelopment, and crime in Walnut Hills, Cincinnati, Ohio. Unpublished doctoral dissertation, University of Cincinnati.

Linning, S.J. & Eck, J.E. (2018). Weak intervention backfire and criminal hormesis: Why some otherwise effective crime prevention interventions can fail at low doses. *The British Journal of Criminology, 58*(2), 309–31.

Lynch, K. (1960). *The image of the city*. Cambridge, MA: MIT press.

MacChesney, N.W. (1927). *The principles of real estate law: Real property, real estate documents and transactions*. New York: The MacMillan Company.

Madensen, T.D. (2007). Bar management and crime: Toward a dynamic theory of place management and crime hotspots. Unpublished doctoral dissertation, University of Cincinnati.

Male, C.T. (1932). *Real estate fundamentals*. New York: D. Van Nostrand Company.

Mallach, A. (2006). *Bringing buildings back: From abandoned properties to community assets*. Montclair, NJ: National Housing Institute.

Manshel, A. (2020). *Learning from Bryant Park: Revitalizing cities, towns, and public spaces*. New Brunswick, NJ: Rutgers University Press.

Martinez, N.N., Lee, Y., Eck, J.E., & O, S. (2017). Ravenous wolves revisited: A systematic review of offending concentration. *Crime Science, 6*(1), 10.

Massey, D.S. & Denton, N.A. (1993). *American apartheid: Segregation and the making of the underclass*. Cambridge, MA: Harvard University Press.

Mawby, R.I. (2017). Defensible space. *Oxford Research Encyclopedia of Criminology*. DOI: 10.1093/acrefore/9780190264079.013.6

Mawby, R.I. (1977). Defensible space: A theoretical and empirical appraisal. *Urban Studies, 14*, 169–79.

Mayhew, P. (1981). Crime in public view: Surveillance and crime prevention. In P.J. Brantingham & P.L. Brantingham (eds.), *Environmental criminology* (pp. 119–43). Prospect Heights, IL: Waveland Press, Inc.

Mayhew, P. (1979). Defensible space: The current status of a crime prevention theory. *The Howard Journal of Penology & Crime Prevention, 18*, 150–9.

Mazerolle, L.G. & Roehl, J. (1998). Civil remedies and crime prevention: An introduction. *Crime Prevention Studies, 9*, 1–18.

Mazerolle, L., Roehl, J., & Kadleck, C. (1998). Controlling social disorder using civil remedies: Results from a randomized field experiment in Oakland,

California. In L. Mazerolle & J. Roehl (eds.), *Crime prevention studies, civil remedies and crime prevention*, Vol. 9 (pp. 141–60). Monsey, NY: Criminal Justice Press.

McMichael, S.L. & Bingham, R.F. (1923). *City growth and values*. Cleveland, OH: The Stanley McMichael Publishing Organization.

McMillen, D., Sarmiento-Barbieri, I., & Singh, R. (2019). Do more eyes on the street reduce crime? Evidence from Chicago's safe passage program. *Journal of Urban Economics*, *110*, 1–25.

Mehlhorn, D. (1998). A requiem for blockbusting: Law, economics, and race-based real estate speculation. *Fordham Law Review*, *67*, 1145.

Merry, S.E. (1981). Defensible space undefended social factors in crime control through environmental design. *Urban Affairs Review*, *16*(4), 397–422.

Miller, N.G. & Markosyan, S. (2003). The academic roots and evolution of real estate appraisal. *The Appraisal Journal*, *71*(2), 172–84.

Mohl, R. (2004). Stop the road: Freeway revolts in American cities. *Journal of Urban History*, *30*(5): 674–706.

Mumford, L. (1962). "Mother Jacobs' Home Remedies." *The New Yorker*. December, p. 148.

Nelson, R.K., Winling, L., Marciano, R., et al. (2020). Mapping Inequality, *American Panorama*. Robert K. Nelson and Edward L. Ayers (eds.). https://dsl.richmond.edu/panorama/redlining

Newman, O. (1973). *Defensible space: Crime prevention through urban design*. New York: MacMillan Publishing.

O, S., Martinez, N.N., Lee, Y., & Eck, J.E. (2017). How concentrated is crime among victims? A systematic review from 1977 to 2014. *Crime Science*, *6*(1), 9.

O'Flaherty, B. (2005). *City economics*. Cambridge, MA: Harvard University Press.

Page, M. (2011). Introduction: More than meets the eye. In M. Page & T. Mennel (eds.), *Reconsidering Jane Jacobs* (pp. 3–14). Chicago, IL: American Planning Association.

Park, R.E. & Burgess, E.W. (1925). *The city*. Chicago, IL: University of Chicago Press.

Payne, T.C. (2010). Does changing ownership change crime? An analysis of apartment ownership and crime in Cincinnati. Unpublished Doctoral Dissertation, University of Cincinnati.

Pearce, D.M. (1979). Gatekeepers and homeseekers: Institutional patterns in racial steering. *Social Problems*, *26*(3), 325–42.

Peiser, R.B. (1997). Real estate development and crime prevention needs. In M. Felson & R.V. Clarke (eds.), *Business and crime prevention* (pp. 231–48). Monsey, NY: Criminal Justice Press.

Pfohl, S. (1994). *Images of deviance and social control: A sociological history.* New York: McGraw-Hill.

Philpott, T.L. (1978). *The slum and the ghetto: Neighborhood deterioration and middle-class reform, Chicago, 1880–1930.* New York: Oxford University Press.

Philadelphia Inquirer (1962, October 23). Writer sees blacklist on Negro home loans. p. 42.

Pickett, S.H. (1968). An appraisal of the urban renewal programme in Canada. *University of Toronto Law Journal, 18*(3), 233–47.

Rabin, Y. (1989). Expulsive zoning: The inequitable legacy of Euclid. In C. M. Harr & J.S. Kayden (eds.), *Zoning and the American dream: Promises still to keep* (pp. 101–21). Chicago, IL: Planners Press, American Planning Association.

Ranasinghe, P. (2011). Jane Jacobs' framing of public disorder and its relation to the "broken windows: theory. *Theoretical Criminology, 16*(1), 63–84.

Ratcliffe, J.H. (2015). Harm-focused policing. Ideas in Policing, #19. Washington, DC: Police Foundation.

Reno, J., Marcus, D., Leary, M.L., & Gist, N.E. (2000). *Keeping illegal activity out of rental property: A police guide for establishing landlord training programs.* Washington, DC: US Department of Justice, Office of Justice Programs.

Reynald, D.M. (2009). Guardianship in action: Developing a new tool for measurement. *Crime Prevention and Community Safety, 11*(1), 1–20.

Rodwin, L. (1961). Neighbors are needed. *New York Times*, p. BR10.

Rogers, A. (2018, June). Major projects in Walnut Hills aim to maintain neighborhood's integrity. *WLWT5 News Cincinnati.* www.wlwt.com/article/major-projects-in-walnut-hills-aim-to-maintain-neighborhoods-integrity/21938640

Rose, C.M. & Brooks, R.W. (2016). Racial covenants and housing segregation, yesterday and today. In A. Brown and V. Smith (eds.), *Race and Real Estate* (pp. 161–76). New York: Oxford University Press.

Rothstein, R. (2017). *The color of law: A forgotten history of how our government segregated America.* New York: Liveright Publishing.

Royal Canadian Mounted Police (2002). Project metrotown: Reducing drug trafficking and related crime through multiagency cooperation and community partnerships. Finalist for 2002 Goldstein Award for Excellence in Problem-Oriented Policing. https://popcenter.asu.edu/sites/default/files/library/awards/goldstein/2002/02-46(F).pdf

Sampson, R.J. (2012). *Great American city: Chicago and the enduring neighborhood effect.* Chicago, IL: The University of Chicago Press.

Sampson, R.J. (2002). Transcending tradition: New direction in community research, Chicago style. *Criminology, 40*, 213–30.

Sampson, R., Eck, J.E., & Dunham, J. (2010). Super controllers and crime prevention: A routine activity explanation of crime prevention success and failure. *Security Journal, 23*(1), 37–51.

Sampson, R.J., Raudenbush, S.W., & Earls, F. (1997). Neighborhoods and violent crime: A multilevel study of collective efficacy. *Science, 277*(5328), 918–24.

Santucci, L. (2019). *How prevalent were racially restrictive covenants in 20th century Philadelphia? A new spatial data set provides answers.* Discussion Paper. Philadelphia, PA: Federal Reserve Bank of Philadelphia.

Satter, B. (2009). *Family properties: Race, real estate, and the exploitation of Black urban Americans.* New York: Metropolitan Books.

Scanlan, A.L. (1949). Racial restrictions in real estate: Property values versus human values. *Notre Dame Law Review, 24*(2), 157–91.

Seattle Civil Rights & Labor History Project. (2020). Racial Restrictive Covenants: Neighborhood by neighborhood restrictions across King County. https://depts.washington.edu/civilr/covenants.htm

Shaw, C.R. & McKay, H.D. (1942/1969). *Juvenile delinquency in urban areas.* Chicago, IL: University of Chicago Press.

Shelley v. Kraemer, 334 U.S. 1, 68 S. Ct. 836 (1948).

Sherman, L.W. (1990). Police crackdowns: Initial and residual deterrence. *Crime and Justice, 12*, 1–48.

Sherman, L.W., Gartin, P.R., & Buerger, M.E. (1989). Hot spots of predatory crime: Routine activities and the criminology of place. *Criminology, 27*(1), 27–56.

Siegel, C. (2016, April 21). The progressive roots of new urbanism. *Public Square: A CNU Journal.* www.cnu.org/publicsquare/progressive-roots-new-urbanism

Silver, C. (1997). The racial origins of zoning in American Cities. In J.M. Thomas & M. Ritzdorf (eds.), *Urban planning and the African American community: In the shadows* (pp. 23–42). Thousand Oaks, CA: Sage.

Skogan, W. (1990). *Disorder and decline: Crime and the spiral of decay in American neighborhoods.* New York: The Free Press.

Smith, M.J. & Clarke, R.V. (2012). Situational crime prevention: Classifying techniques using "good enough" theory. In B.C. Welsh & D.P. Farrington (eds.), *The Oxford handbook of crime prevention* (pp. 291–315). New York: Oxford University Press.

Snodgrass, J. (1976). Clifford R. Shaw and Henry D. McKay: Chicago criminologists. *The British Journal of Criminology, 16*(1), 1–19.

Sobel, R. (1989). *Trammell Crow, master builder: The story of America's largest real estate empire.* Hoboken, NJ: John Wiley & Sons.

Somin, I. & Getman, R.S. (2004, December). Brief of Jane Jacobs as *Amica Curiae* in support of petitioners regarding *Kelo v. City of New London,* submitted to the Supreme Court of the United States (no. 04–108). http://www.ij.org/images/pdf_folder/private_property/kelo/jacobs05.pdf

Suarez, R. (2011). Ric Burns New York documentary, Episode 7, 59–60min, Public Broadcasting Service (PBS).

Sugrue, T.J. (1995). Crabgrass-roots politics: Race, rights, and the reaction against Liberalism in the Urban North, 1940–1964. *The Journal of American History, 82*(2), 551–78.

Swartsell, N. (2017, November 17). What's in Mayor Cranley's offer to FC Cincinnati? *City Beat.* www.citybeat.com/news/blog/20983304/whats-in-mayor-cranleys-offer-to-fc-cincinnati

Taylor, R.B. (2015). *Community criminology: Fundamentals of spatial and temporal scaling, ecological indicators, and selectivity bias.* New York: New York University Press.

Taylor, R.B. & Gottfredson, S.D. (1986). Environmental design, crime, and prevention: An examination of community dynamics. *Crime and Justice, 8,* 387–416.

Taylor, R.B., Gottfredson, S.D., & Brower, S. (1981). Territorial cognitions and prevention: An examination of community dynamics. *Crime and Justice, 8,* 387–416.

Taylor, R.B., Koons, B.A., Kurtz, E.M., Greene, J.R., & Perkins, D.D. (1995). Street blocks with more nonresidential land use have more physical deterioration: Evidence from Baltimore and Philadelphia. *Urban Affairs Review, 31*(1), 120–36.

Teaford, J. (1990). *The rough road to renaissance: Urban revitalization in America, 1940–1985.* Baltimore, MD: Johns Hopkins University Press.

Tillyer, M.S., Wilcox, P., & Walter, R.J. (2021). Crime generators in context: examining "place in neighborhood" propositions. *Journal of Quantitative Criminology, 37,* 517–46.

Trounstine, J. (2018). *Segregation by design: Local politics and inequality in American cities.* New York: Cambridge University Press.

Tweh, B. (2016). $10M Walnut Hills development ready to open. *The Enquirer:* Cincinnati. www.cincinnati.com/story/money/2016/01/15/walnut-hills-trevarren-flats/77763278/

Unnever, J.D. (1987). Reviewed works: The social ecology of crime. *Contemporary Sociology, 16*(6), 845–6.

Unnever, J.D., Cullen, F.T., Mathers, S.A., McClure, T.E., & Allison, M.C. (2009). Racial discrimination and Hirschi's criminological classic: A chapter in the sociology of knowledge. *Justice Quarterly, 26*(3), 377–409.

Venkatesh, S. (2001). Chicago's pragmatic planners. *Social Science History, 2,* 275–317.

Wagers, M., Sousa, W., & Kelling, G. (2017). Broken windows. In R. Wortley & M. Townsley (eds.), *Environmental criminology and crime analysis,* 2nd ed. (pp. 334–50). New York: Routledge.

Warerkar, T. (2018, September 14). New York's 10 biggest property owners: See all the key players in New York's real estate scene and to what extent they control the city's landscape. Curbed New York. https://ny.curbed.com/2018/9/14/17860172/new-york-10-biggest-property-owners

Weber, J. (2012). The evolving Interstate Highway System and the changing geography of the United States. *Journal of Transport Geography, 25,* 70–86.

Weimer, A. & Hoyt, H. (1948). *Principles of urban real estate,* 2nd ed. New York: The Ronald Press Company.

Weimer, A. & Hoyt, H. (1939). *Principles of urban real estate,* 1st ed. New York: The Ronald Press Company.

Weingroff, R.F. (1996). Federal-aid highway act of 1956: Creating the interstate system. *Public Roads, 60*(1). www.fhwa.dot.gov/publications/publicroads/96summer/p96su10.cfm

Weisburd, D. (2015). The law of crime concentration and the criminology of place. *Criminology, 53*(2), 133–57.

Weisburd, D., Bushway, S., Lum, C., & Yang, S. M. (2004). Trajectories of crime at places: A longitudinal study of street segments in the city of Seattle. *Criminology, 42*(2), 283–322.

Weisburd, D., Eck, J.E., Braga, A.A., et al. (2016). *Place matters: Criminology for the twenty-first century.* New York: Cambridge University Press.

Weisburd, D., Gill, C., Wooditch, A., Barritt, W., & Murphy, J. (2021a). Building collective action at crime hot spots: Findings from a randomized field experiment. *Journal of Experimental Criminology, 17,* 161–91.

Weisburd, D., Groff, E.R., & Yang, S.M. (2012). *The criminology of place: Street segments and our understanding of the crime problem.* New York: Oxford University Press.

Weisburd, D., White, C., Wire, S., & Wilson, D.B. (2021b). Enhancing informal social controls to reduce crime: Evidence from a study of crime hot spots. Prevention Science, *22*(4), 509–22.

Weisburd, D., Wyckoff, L.A., Ready, J., et al. (2006). Does crime just move around the corner? A controlled study of spatial displacement and diffusion of crime control benefits. *Criminology, 44*(3), 549–91.

Whittemore, A.H. (2012). How the Federal government zoned America: The Federal housing administration and zoning. *Journal of Urban History, 39*(4), 620–42.

WHRF. (2016). Walnut Hills Reinvestment Plan. www.dropbox.com/s/3zcj80nkk43fii3/c15702RptBook161101finalx3.pdf?dl=0

Wilcox, P., Cullen, F.T., & Feldmeyer, B. (2018). *Communities and crime: An enduring American challenge.* Philadelphia, PA: Temple University Press.

Wilcox, P. & Eck, J.E. (2011). Criminology of the unpopular. *Criminology & Public Policy, 10*(2), 473–82.

Wilcox, P., Quisenberry, N., Cabrera, D.T., & Jones, S. (2004). Busy places and broken windows? Toward defining the role of physical structure and process in community crime models. *The Sociological Quarterly, 45*(2), 185–207.

Wilcox, P. & Tillyer, M.S. (2018). Place and neighborhood contexts. In D. Weisburd & J.E. Eck (eds.), *Unraveling the crime-place connection: New directions in theory and policy* (pp. 121–42). New York: Routledge.

Wilson, J.Q. & Kelling, G.L. (1982). Broken windows: The police and neighborhood safety. *The Atlantic Monthly*, March, 29–38.

Woodard, C. (2016, June 16). How Cincinnati salvaged the nation's most dangerous neighborhood: Leaning on the power of local corporations, officials engineered a renaissance's in the city's heart. *Politico Magazine.* www.politico.com/magazine/story/2016/06/what-works-cincinnati-ohio-over-the-rhine-crime-neighborhood-turnaround-city-urban-revitalization-213969

Wortley, R. & Townsley, M. (2016). Environmental criminology and crime analysis: Situating the theory, analytic approach and application. In R. Wortley & M. Townsley (eds.), *Environmental criminology and crime analysis* (pp. 1–25). New York: Routledge.

Wright, K. & Nickol, J. (2016). *The neighborhood playbook: Activating spaces, developing places.* Covington, KY: Yard & Company.

Zidar, M.S., Shafer, J.G., & Eck, J.E. (2018). Reframing an obvious police problem: Discovery, analysis and response to a manufactured problem in a small city. *Policing: A Journal of Policy and Practice, 12*(3), 316–31.

Zipp, S. & Storring, N. (2017). Part two: City building, 1952–1965. In S. Zipp & N. Storring (eds.), *Vital little plans: The short works of Jane Jacobs* (pp. 37–43). New York: Random House.

Acknowledgments

We thank the people who provided us with invaluable feedback at various stages of writing this Element. Dr. Francis Cullen, Dr. Ben Feldmeyer, Dr. Ajima Olaghere, and Police Captain Daniel Gerard (Ret.) gave us helpful suggestions on an initial draft of the manuscript. Dr. J.C. Barnes, Dr. Kate Bowers, and Dr. Pamela Wilcox commented on earlier versions of our second and fourth sections. Dr. David Weisburd and two anonymous reviewers provided very thoughtful reviews that improved our manuscript. We are extremely grateful to have so many colleagues give us their time and feedback. Their comments helped us strengthen our arguments and sharpen our writing.

Cambridge Elements ☰

Criminology

David Weisburd
George Mason University, Virginia

Advisory Board

About the series

Elements in Criminology seeks to identify key contributions in theory and empirical research that help to identify, enable, and stake out advances in contemporary criminology. The series will focus on radical new ways of understanding and framing criminology, whether of place, communities, persons, or situations. The relevance of criminology for preventing and controlling crime will also be a key focus of this series.

Cambridge Elements ≡

Criminology

Elements in the series

CPSIA information can be obtained
at www.ICGtesting.com
Printed in the USA
LVHW050030011221
704822LV00011B/840